7000443176

University of the
West of England

BRISTOL

Library Services
UWE, Bristol
Glenside Campus
Blackberry Hill
Stapleton
Bristol BS16 1DD

Please ensure that this book is returned by the end of
the loan period for which it is issued.

UWE, BRISTOL   9187A.08.04
Printing & Stationery Services

27 MAY 2009

Library Web Address: http://www.uwe.ac.uk/library/

305.26019 WAR

305.
6
AR

Research

CW01572383

heway

NUMBER 8 IN

**THE REPRESENTATION OF OLDER PEOPLE
IN AGEING RESEARCH SERIES**

THE CENTRE FOR POLICY ON AGEING AND
THE CENTRE FOR AGEING AND BIOGRAPHICAL
STUDIES AT THE OPEN UNIVERSITY

SERIES EDITORS
SHEILA PEACE AND JOANNA BORNAT

C|P|A

The Open
University

First published in 2008
by the Centre for Policy on Ageing
25–31 Ironmonger Row
London EC1V 3QP
Tel: +44 (0)20 7553 6500
Fax: +44 (0)20 7553 6501
Email: cpa@cpa.org.uk
Website: www.cpa.org.uk
Registered charity no 207163

© 2008 Centre for Policy on Ageing
British Library Cataloguing in Publication Data
A catalogue record for this book is available from the British Library
ISBN 978-1-901097-11-5
All rights reserved. No part of this publication may be reproduced or
transmitted in any form by any means, without the prior consent of the
copyright owner.

The Representation of Older People in Ageing Research Series is based on
seminars organised by the Centre for Ageing and Biographical Studies,
Faculty of Health and Social Care, the Open University, and the Centre for
Policy on Ageing. The papers in this volume have been revised since the
seminar took place.

Titles in the series:

Printed in the United Kingdom by Henry Ling Limited,
at the Dorset Press, Dorchester DT1 1HD

CONTENTS

iii

RESEARCHING AGE AND MULTIPLE DISCRIMINATION
Introduction

RICHARD WARD AND BILL BYTHEWAY

In social gerontology the current debate on age discrimination (Macnicol 2006) seems set on a low flame. It simmers away as an adjunct to much on-going research, but rarely boils over as an issue demanding urgent attention. The systematic gathering of evidence in the UK has been limited, and relates mainly to employment practices and the job market (Glover and Branine 2001). The result is that many assumptions about ageism rest upon a better knowledge of other forms of prejudice. All too often, for example, ageism is introduced as something that is 'equivalent to' sexism and racism. This assumption raises the important question as to whether one area of discrimination is knowable through another – are the 'isms' essentially the same? Or does each relate to a distinct form of discrimination? Without a more informed and critical understanding of how older people experience discrimination, we have to question how certain we can be of those remedies that might be proposed for tackling ageism.

Vital questions regarding the significance of discrimination in later life therefore remain, and approaches to both understanding and demonstrating the relationships between the various inequalities that might place older people at a disadvantage are still to be worked out. To date, for example, in explaining multiple discrimination, much faith has been placed in the expediency of adding one form of discrimination to another, e.g. ageism + sexism = double jeopardy (Sontag 1972). The debate on prejudice is strewn with notions of double and triple whammies and penalties, and there has been little concern to unpack the synergistic nature of multiple discrimination.

This collection of papers originates in a seminar held on 15 March 2006 under the title 'Age-old prejudices: research with older people in a discriminatory world'. It was the eighth in the series 'Representation of Older People in Ageing Research' organised by the Centre for Policy on Ageing and the Centre for Ageing and

Biographical Studies at the Open University. The aim of the seminar was to explore how older people encounter discrimination, and the processes involved in researching such experiences.

Three of the four papers report on research undertaken in association with the RoAD (Research on Age Discrimination) project, a participative study of older people's accounts of age discrimination (Bytheway *et al.* 2007). For this reason, much of what follows explores how older people report the experience of discrimination, and how they respond to, and make sense of, this. Covering the whole of the UK, the RoAD project is, we believe, the first instance of research with the primary objective of gathering evidence of age discrimination, wherever, whenever and however it might occur. The findings, including those reported in the papers collected here, are therefore crucial to an understanding of the systemic nature of age discrimination and the ways it is reproduced. Each of these papers provides evidence of how everyday experience contributes to the way discrimination is understood, defined and perceived by older people.

In Chapter 2, RoAD researchers draw attention to the shifting sands of racism in northern England underlining its processual quality and intersections with different points in the life course. The narratives on offer show how inequalities and bias accumulate in people's lives, and where better to discover the long-term implications of living with discrimination than through asking and listening to older people.

In their study of older women's experiences of hairdressing (Chapter 3), Symonds and Holland offer a poignant example of the way day-to-day encounters are embedded with intersecting patterns of discrimination. The authors outline the divisions and exclusions associated with the hairdressing industry. It is well known to be a gendered service, with individual shops targeting people according to budget and age. The study was triggered by an 87-year-old woman's account of refusing an OAP discount in an attempt to avoid the imposition of a uniform 'pensioner's hairdo'. She discovered that the way in which older women are served is markedly different to that enjoyed by younger customers. What Symonds and Holland reveal is how social divisions on the basis of age are subtly reproduced, in this case via the embodied practice of hairdressing.

Chapter 4 draws on interviews with men and women, exploring how age discrimination constrains sexual behaviour and the representation of sexual identities. Interviewees in this study described experiences as diverse as night-clubbing, visiting the doctor, interactions with neighbours, shopping on the high street and pension entitlement. Integral to an understanding of discrimination is seeing how such varied experiences combine to place older people at a disadvantage.

In Chapter 5, Sin anticipates the establishment of the Commission for Equality and Human Rights and the implications of upcoming policy on discrimination for campaigners and, in particular, for the Disability Rights Commission. He considers the complexities behind the categories of 'disabled' and 'old', contrasting the fixed and rigid definitions relied upon in policy with the fluid quality of everyday identities.

Finally in the concluding Chapter 6, we argue that these studies draw attention to the contingent nature of discrimination and associated identities or positionings. In contrast to the great act of disentanglement currently underway in formulating anti-discrimination policy, this research underlines how age interconnects with the various strands to which the legislation refers. Identities are 'en-aged' while age is culturally produced and reiterated in ways that are shaped by time and place, such that the experience of growing old is complex and diverse. As a result generalising attributions are problematic. Currently, one certainty that does exist is the knowledge that ageism underpins much of the discrimination that remains a feature of all our lives.

REFERENCES

Bytheway, B., Ward, R., Holland, C.A. and Peace, S.M. (2007) *Too Old: Older People's Accounts of Discrimination, Exclusion and Rejection*, London: Help the Aged.

Glover, I. and Branine, M. (2001) *Ageism in Work and Employment*, Aldershot: Ashgate.

Macnicol, J. (2006) *Age Discrimination: An Historical and Contemporary Analysis*, Cambridge: Cambridge University Press.

Sontag, S. (1972) The double standard of ageing, *Saturday Review*, 23, 29–38.

2

LIFETIMES OF DISCRIMINATION
The experiences of older members of three ethnic minority communities

THE RESEARCH ON AGE DISCRIMINATION PROJECT (RoAD)[1]

INTRODUCTION

This chapter draws on two interconnected studies undertaken as part of the RoAD project in the neighbouring cities of Bradford and Leeds. Despite consulting with older people via a large network of groups and forums across the UK, the RoAD team realised the standpoints of black and minority ethnic older people were under-represented. This suggested that networks in old age are often culturally and racially divided and meant that much of the evidence being gathered was skewed toward the perspectives of the ethnic majority. Both the Bradford and Leeds studies therefore aimed to generate accounts of the experience of discrimination related by older members of minority communities. One aim was to hear how age discrimination overlaps with experiences of racism in everyday life. Discussions with three different groups also allowed comparisons between the narratives of older migrants who share the experience of ageing during a period in which many northern towns and cities were transformed by Britain's shift to a post-industrial society.

Migration, ageing and discrimination

There are many reasons why it is important to think about age when considering the particular experiences of discrimination faced by migrant communities. Migration is a selective process commonly weighted towards younger members. Indeed, age bars are often a

---

[1] Research for this chapter was carried out by Ulfat Riaz in Bradford and Jenny Sleight and Zara Farshi in Leeds (see their more detailed reports, which are numbers 6 and 7 on http://road.open.ac.uk/reports.htm).

decisive element of the criteria used to control entry to many developed nations. Migration is also a gendered process; traditionally (work-aged) men have migrated first before sending for their families, whereas more recently the growth of service sector industries has led to women migrants (to developed nations) outnumbering men (McKibbin 2006; Sharpe 2001). This means that successive generations of migrant communities have faced a gender imbalance often compounded by ever-tightening immigration controls. Also significant differences exist between first generation migrants and those born in the UK. As the authors of one study argued:

> The older generation express what we would term 'denizen identities': they feel that their presence in Britain is not one of a citizenship 'right', and consequently the younger generation see them, and the first generation migrants feel themselves, as not having a legitimate voice. They feel they lack the 'full citizenship' of their sons and daughters and the political rights associated with it.
>
> (Hussain and Bagguley 2005: 418)

Such a perspective is significant when we seek to elicit accounts of discrimination, as it raises questions of whether the lack of a political voice shapes interpretations and responses to such experiences. For instance, are the older members of migrant communities in Bradford and Leeds more accommodating or tolerant of discrimination as a result of this putatively 'denizen' identity?

All the participants in both cities had lived in the UK for over 40 years. Most arrived in Britain in the late 1950s and early 1960s and prior to the 1971 Immigration Act, which sought to control the entry of men seeking work from the Commonwealth and Pakistan as well as limiting 'secondary immigration' i.e. for the purpose of family reunification. Despite formal encouragement to migrate to Britain (via the British Nationality Act 1948) in order to meet the labour needs of a burgeoning post-war health service, transport infrastructure and industrial growth, migrants faced widespread discrimination and suspicion. It was common for migrant workers to find themselves unable to use the skills, training and qualifications acquired in their country of origin and thereby face downward social mobility upon arrival (Platt 2007). Migrants were concentrated in unskilled areas of employment with few rights. Consequently they were the section of the workforce most vulnerable to unemployment. Low income and lack of resources also meant many faced poor housing conditions in deprived areas with restricted access to welfare services and support.

A study by Valentine and McDonald (2004) found that prejudice against migrants is often couched in economic rather than cultural terms but varies according to local conditions. Differing socio-economic factors were found to influence the discrimination expressed toward migrant communities. In areas with high unemployment, migrants were the targets of blame for taking jobs from indigenous workers whereas, in smaller rural settings, fears were expressed that 'outsiders' would bring crime and cause disruption. The study also found that visibility in public space is crucial to arguments about the perceived cultural threat posed by minority groups, often signalled in terms such as 'invasion', 'taking over' and 'swamping', as employed regularly in the media and political discourses on immigration. Findings such as these suggest it is important to recognise the role played by time and place when examining and analysing discrimination.

Evidence also indicates that 'migrant' is not a homogeneous category; different groups and communities fare differently for complex reasons. For instance Platt (2007) notes the particularly hostile discrimination faced by African-Caribbean migrants, citing evidence of their contrasting experiences of social mobility compared to other minority groups. As this chapter goes on to explore, the experience of discrimination is also age-related. Not only do older migrants face age discrimination as older people, different forms of discrimination emerge at certain life stages and may affect one generation differently from the next. For instance, Hussain and Bagguley (2005) emphasise that racism can be premised not only on skin colour, pointing out that lack of fluency in English can give rise to negative stereotyping. For many communities, proficiency in English divides older and younger generations with British-born sons and daughters acting as translators for their parents, assisting them with access to the welfare state and other resources. Another contrast between older and younger generations is the experience of cumulative disadvantage that compounds inequalities in later life

6

(O'Rand 1996). Persistent exposure to racism throughout the life course is integral to the cumulative quality of disadvantage and a key consideration in regard to ageing and discrimination (Sin 2005).

The two studies

In Bradford, four focus groups were held with members of the Pakistani community; two with women, two with men, and followed up by six in-depth interviews with attendees of a local Pakistani community centre. Discussions took place in Punjabi, Pushto or Urdu and were subsequently translated and transcribed by the facilitator. In Leeds, focus group discussions were conducted with six members of a lunch club for the African-Caribbean community; seven members of a social services day centre, also largely serving the African-Caribbean community; and six users of a project offering support services for Irish people. Each centre was visited beforehand by the facilitators who explained the purpose and nature of the research.

As we discuss below, the two studies generated very different types of information and evidence of discrimination. One focused largely on past experiences and illustrated how these are made sense of and reflected upon in later life. The other project looked at on-going contemporary experiences, much of which involves what Amin (2002) has described as 'the daily negotiations of ethnic difference'. These differing emphases are significant because they underline the generative quality of the research process and the importance of attending to it. One notable contrast between the projects was that the facilitator for the Bradford study is a member of the Pakistani community whereas neither facilitator of the Leeds study are members of the communities that the participants belonged to. We can only speculate upon the influences this dynamic might have had upon the recounting of experiences.

Sin (2005) recalls a host of concerns over the process of research when exploring experiences of discrimination with older people from black and minority ethnic groups. For instance, he highlights the difficulties associated with articulating ambiguous incidents under conditions where evidence of discrimination is being sought. Questions also exist over how differences in definitions and understandings are handled; it cannot be assumed that each person defines racism or age discrimination in the same way. Another

7

important consideration for the projects detailed below was the use of discussion groups to generate accounts. The research relied upon people's ability to recall and recount discriminatory experiences. It was also assumed that participants would be prepared to talk about discrimination and/or present themselves as subject to it, in a group setting.

In retrospect, it is clear that a focus on gathering 'evidence' by way of examples and recounted experiences meant less emphasis on explanations of 'why' or 'how' participants came to view certain experiences as discriminatory and others as not. Essed (1991) argues that the process of interpreting a particular experience is tied to a wider comprehension of discrimination based on past experiences. In a group context, it may for instance, be interesting and helpful to consider how certain accounts generate nods of agreement while others raise a laugh, or cases where other group members distance themselves from a comment. Such processes reveal both individual and group levels of understanding and potentially illustrate how groups and communities work up certain perceptions and understandings of discrimination – supporting some perspectives while silencing others.

One benefit associated with incorporating the comments and perspectives of more than one group is the added element of comparison it affords. This chapter therefore offers an indication of what discrimination means and how it is discussed and understood at the level of particular communities but also how this process compares across different communities. Alongside this, insights are offered into experiences of discrimination at a particular point in time and place. Variations in the nature of discrimination are made apparent and how concerns/beliefs are tied to local conditions and circumstances as well as to certain groups and communities are signalled. Thus, rather than seeking to arrive at generalisations or summations, this chapter considers the experiences of a particular generation of migrants who have aged in northern towns and cities during the last half of the twentieth century. The importance of understanding the complexity of discrimination in context is therefore underlined.

THE PAKISTANI COMMUNITY IN BRADFORD

The Bradford riots of 2001 drew national attention to the area and to the local Pakistani community especially. Media coverage referred to 'ghettoes of the north' and 'no-go areas' (cited in Webster 2003), while official reports on the riots noted 'white flight' from inner urban areas that had reportedly created racially segregated housing and education (cited in Hussain and Bagguley 2005). Kundnani (2001) notes the aftermath of the riots led to the professionalisation of a small number of spokespersons who entered the town halls of Bradford and Oldham as authoritative representatives for their broader communities. The media also placed emphasis on generational tensions within the Pakistani community, the inference being that older members of the community had lost control of younger generations who, in turn, had lost respect for their elders.

Most of the men interviewed in Bradford came to the UK in the 1950s and 1960s when they were in their twenties and thirties. Many initially assumed that their stay in Britain would be temporary and that they would return to Pakistan better off than when they left. However, in reality many could barely afford to live on their wages, and what little they had was sent to their families back home. Descriptions of the commitments by which they were bound signalled the complex system of duties and reciprocity of networks that stretch from the UK to Pakistan. While compounding the financial burden faced by many, these links serve as a crucial means of support and assistance and play a key role in the survival and progress made by migrants.

Abdul Khadiq, 73, remembers his early adult life:

I came to England in the 1960s and worked in Nottingham for a plasterboard company earning about £7.50 per week. I worked 12 to 15 hours a day and took any overtime work that came up. It was really difficult making ends meet because I was trying to live some sort of life here and ensure that my family was looked after back home. I had a lot of responsibility on my shoulders and it was awful.

Several men talked about the debts they had incurred in travelling to the UK. Many were unqualified when they arrived, and relied on help from relatives to get work. Here is how Majid Ali, aged 70, described his arrival:

> *I came to England in 1963 with some family. My two brothers were already here and they sent the money to get me over. As soon as I came over, my brother got me a job working with him in a textile mill. It was such hard work, the long hours and the sleeping arrangements in the house were awful. Ten of us shared a house, and my brother's wife was over. She did all the cooking and cleaning. The money we earned went into a single pot and we saved enough money to pay the deposit for a house that we would share.*

This quote also gives some insight into the gendered arrangements of migrant households, in this case with one woman supporting nine men. Sharpe (2001) argues that the community-building role played by women is often overlooked or underplayed in histories of migrant communities.

Unemployment and work

Across the UK, employment statistics consistently reveal that black and minority ethnic groups fare differently within the employment market in comparison to white groups. Ethnic minority groups are generally more likely to be unemployed than the white group across all ages (Summerfield and Babb 2003), but differences also exist between the groups. Unemployment statistics for black and minority ethnic communities also highlight their greater vulnerability within the employment market during periods of high unemployment (Sly 1994). There is a long-standing history to this vulnerability and as participants in the Bradford project revealed, it is a situation often compounded by age, with opportunities for retraining and re-employment becoming ever more restricted.

The collapse of the textile industry in the 1980s left many respondents living in Bradford and out of work. On applying for jobs, many were told they were 'too old' and those who did find work often had to work very long hours or even hold down two jobs in order to carry on taking care of their families in Pakistan. Typical occupations included driving taxis or working in takeaways. Bibi Shanas, a 63-year-old widow, described the plight of her late husband:

My husband was uneducated and when the mills closed down he was unemployed for many years. No matter how hard he tried he could not get any work, except in takeaways where, at times, he would get paid £5 per night from 4pm till 2am. Only after six months did that go up a bit. He was always told that he was too old to work.

The scarcity of jobs meant that employers could pick and choose the type of staff they wanted and get away with providing poor working conditions, as Hamza, 75, explained:

There was no loyalty with our employers, they knew we needed these jobs and used it against us by paying us low wages, no sick pay and holidays. I hated being made to feel like this. Back home I was educated and felt like I was somebody. I went to school in Pakistan and would have gone on to college, but my father saw an opportunity for me to come to England, thinking it would be good for me.

Fazwel Hussain, 71, described the cumulative effect of poor working conditions on his health:

In my later years I suffered from back pain, from lifting heavy boxes and bales of wool, and loss of hearing due to the noise of the machinery, bronchial illness due to the chemicals we worked with in the mills. We were never compensated.

Racial discrimination

Many described the racial discrimination they encountered when arriving in Britain. Majid Ali said:

When I came here I was shocked by the racism and discrimination we experienced on a daily basis. I remember going to the park with my friends and the white folk wouldn't sit on the same bench as us.

Such prejudice affected their attempts to gain jobs outside the textile industry. Haji Mahmood, aged 67, remembered:

We were told to get back to our factories and called dirty names. It was a difficult period, and when we lost our jobs and had to

11

sign on we were called nakam, *plus whatever other dirty words came to some of the white people.*

Racism affected other aspects of their lives. Bibi Shanas spoke for many older women when describing the problems she had in obtaining welfare benefits:

When my husband passed away it took forever to get my benefits sorted out. At one point they said he has never paid any National Insurance contribution. The benefit office was no help, I didn't have the language skills and the interpreter they used was more interested in me leaving than sorting my stuff out. He felt embarrassed as I was unable to answer their questions. I finally had to find someone to sort it out for me at the local community centre.

Discrimination in relation to both age and race underlies the following comment by Haji Mohammed Gulzar:

I haven't worked since 1985. I am too old and poorly to work now, but when I had the health and the desire to work I wasn't given the opportunity.

Age was also an element in some of the women's experiences of racial discrimination. For example, when having children in her thirties, Shazia Manzoor commented that hospital nurses had said she was 'too old' and should stop:

But back home women were having babies in their thirties and forties. Nothing happened to them. But I guess they [the nurses] never said that to the women from their own white community.

Now in later life, the women considered their community centre a good place to meet other women, but felt that the facilities and opportunities available to older women were generally poor and that, compared with younger women, they were not given equal access to social events and activities. Riaza Bibi, aged 60, commented:

We get taken out on trips and things but it's not the same as having say English classes, or being taken swimming on a regular basis, going away on residentials and trips abroad. We know that the centre has many facilities for young people but we are unable to access them because they say they have age

*restrictions on them. We might be old but we still want to do
things and see the world, but staff just assume that we wouldn't
want to do these things because of our age. In fact, it's the
opposite. I want to do as much as I can, to have a social life, go
on trips, visit new places and even go to France and Spain. This
is what I would love the centre to do for us.*

Age discrimination

Most respondents first become aware of age discrimination when
they became unemployed in the 1980s. Many could not speak fluent
English and had no formal qualifications or training. Little if any
language and literacy support was available either from employers or
local education authorities. Haji Mohammed Gulzar again offers a
telling account:

*After 1975, because the mills were closing down, I never found
any work. I was only 43. Because I had no qualifications and
couldn't speak English, I couldn't get a job. Any jobs that I did
get were very short-term, a few weeks here and there. I only got
these jobs because my friends and family used to put in a good
word for me.*

Age discrimination also created other obstacles. Fazel Hussain
described the problems he faced in applying for his daughters to join
him in the UK:

*I always worked in the mills and also worked as a taxi driver.
When finally I had saved enough money I applied to have my
two daughters come to the UK. They were turned down because
the British Embassy said they were too old, one was 16 and the
other 17, it was awful. That to me is what age discrimination is
about. When do children not need their parents?*

Such bureaucratic rulings offer an insight into the racialised
dimension of mobility that Richmond (1994) has described as the
imposition of 'global apartheid' by developed nations. Some
respondents spoke of feeling humiliated by the attempts of the
authorities to establish the age of children who did not have birth
certificates. Sufi Ali Shah, 68, provided another example of the effect
of age discrimination:

13

Many years I have lived in this country and worked hard, paid my taxes and the rest. About eight years ago my wife passed away. I went back to Pakistan about two years ago and met a woman and we got married. I have tried to bring my wife over to the UK but they refused my sponsorship because, they said, I was on a pension and therefore not working and could not support her. So I have started to look for work, when I go to agencies and tell them I want to work with them they think I am joking, but I have been trying to find work for the last year and so far no luck. The whole system is set up to fail people that are over a certain age, and even more if you don't have the language. I tried to go back to Pakistan and live there but my grandchildren and children are all here and I am torn, especially since their mum passed away. I am all they have.

This story encapsulates the complex ways in which bureaucratic restrictions on migration and employment are intertwined with everyday age and racial prejudice.

Generational tensions

Izzat, meaning honour, is a powerful concept in Pakistan and an integral part of family life. Shaw (2000) notes that *izzat* applies particularly to the conduct of women. Their identities are most affected by questions of honour because women play a major role in the relations of informal reciprocity in Pakistani communities. Thus, the fulfilment of obligations towards kin has greater consequences for the moral identities of women than men (Ahmad 2002). Many respondents referred to their children's families, and the importance of being shown *izzat* by them. Others also mentioned the importance of this aspect of Asian life, as illustrated by this comment from a Caribbean-born participant in one of the Leeds focus groups:

I [live] among what you would call the Asian community. I would like to live among them if I could until I die, because as far as age is concerned ... they are a respectful generation.

Despite this, some Bradford participants (particularly women) painted a more complex and darker picture of family life, citing examples of older women, despite being ill-treated by younger members of the family, refusing to complain on the grounds that this

14

would bring dishonour to the family. Ahmad (2002) notes that tensions and conflicts between mothers-in-law and daughters-in-law are 'legendary' in Pakistani communities, not least as a result of the tradition for newly-weds to reside in the husband's family home. Two interviewees were prepared to share their stories. Zora Shaheen, 67, spoke of a turbulent and sometimes violent relationship with her daughter-in-law:

> *I was made a widow 10 years ago, my husband was a good man and my son is a good lad, but I can't say the same for his wife. They live with me, she has three children who I love very much but they are naughty. My son works long hours and that means me and his wife are home a lot. She makes me angry, every single day we fight, we argue and one time she hit me. I called the police and they locked her up for the night. A week later she fought with me again and I hit her. She called the police and they locked me up for the night. The whole community was in uproar. Her children are allowed to mess my stuff around, she even tried to make me sign the house over to her and my son. Not on my dead body will she ever get anything from me. I thought about moving out, but then thought against it, why should I move out? It's my house. But I won't kick them out, I love my son. But he never takes sides.*

Another participant revealed that her daughter-in-law had threatened to leave, telling her she would never see her son and grandchildren again. Others described being asked to sign over the house, land, money, jewellery and even the pension book. Another said she was made fun of and threatened with being sent to an old people's home 'like the white people do'. Others talked of being sworn at and called names such as *budhee* (old woman) or *pahgal* (mad).

Men also expressed concerns about *izzat* and their relations with younger members of their own families. Fazel Hussain, now turned 70, feels well looked after and dismisses the idea of age discrimination. However, he retired as a taxi driver at the behest of his children: 'It was only last year when I turned 70 that my kids put a stop to me working.'

THE AFRICAN/CARIBBEAN AND IRISH
COMMUNITIES IN LEEDS

There are many similarities between the evidence gathered in Leeds and Bradford but also some significant differences. The Bradford focus groups concentrated on memories of past discrimination and the contemporary cultural values of today's Pakistani communities. In facilitating the Leeds focus groups the researchers raised issues concerning current experiences of discrimination and, in particular, the interplay between ageist and racist prejudice.

In regard to Irish people, there is a long history of 'racialisation' by the English, stretching back to the Victorian era. The cultural markers of this prejudice: drunkenness, dirtiness, laziness and violence, have supported pervasive and institutionalised discrimination. This history provides evidence that those conceptions of racial difference based exclusively on skin colour are unnecessarily limited (Popoviciu and Mac an Ghaill 2004).

Age and racial discrimination

Ingrid, a focus group participant, provided a detailed description of an incident which illustrates how older people from minority communities can experience segregation, and how they interpret the complex relationship between age and racial discrimination:

> *Yesterday, in the swimming pool, this white lady she is swimming like she owns the pool. Now I am a small person as you will see. When I'm in the pool I love for my feet to touch the floor. Anyway, I was in front of this young woman and she is coming and coming, swimming on her back. I was just right at the beginning of the bottom end of the pool, the six feet part, and I felt like I was going under so I held on to the rope that they have there for protection and I just looked at her and I says: 'Can't you swim properly? I don't like people swimming like that.'*

> *Now everybody in the pool knows me, this is the first time I have ever seen her in the pool. So she says: 'You don't say nothing, if you can't keep quiet, go out.' You know what she said to me? 'If you don't like it and you can't swim, you should be above there with them.' Now above there with them is all the black people,*

16

with a few older people, that just come in. I have never seen them before. I am the only black person that swims below there because the pool assistants, they always say to me, 'you swim below because you are a good swimmer'. [...]

That was discrimination [...] in my view I looked like I was the oldest person in the pool, number one, and number two, I were black and she felt that I shouldn't have any right swimming below there because all the white people were below there and the black ones all above. But don't get me wrong, those that were black above there, can't swim, they were wearing the arm bands and learning things. So to me that's discrimination.

A significant aspect of this account is Ingrid's understanding of the two forms of discrimination and how the account is set out in a way that shows her own process of interpreting the encounter: 'number one' she was old; and 'number two' she was black. It is a narrative that reveals the way discrimination inhabits routine social encounters in public spaces and as such offers an indication of discrimination as an everyday experience.

Tolerating prejudice?

As with the groups in Bradford, all the participants in the Leeds focus groups had experienced race discrimination since gaining entry to the UK. A discussion involving Doris and Alma, two residents of a sheltered housing scheme, demonstrates how racial prejudice has persisted:

Doris: Where I am living now, we have an old lady living next door to me. When the children come to see me, you know like in the summer and they lay out on the grass, she will go to her window and say 'Go back to Chapeltown [an area of Leeds with a high black and minority ethnic population].' I mentioned to the warden one day that sometimes she does throw toilet rolls outside to the back after she's finished with them ... The warden says, 'Oh no, she wouldn't do a thing like that.' Head office say, 'Just ignore her, she seem to be going funny.'

Alma: We will never get rid of this racism. Like coming up here this morning, she would see me and say, 'Oh get out, get out to

Chapeltown where you come from.' Sometimes it gets me down a bit but they tell me not to bother with her. I would like to enjoy my pension with ease, not for people to pass remarks on me because I am black, because I live next door to them. I don't like it, but I have to put up with it. I just leave them alone because you are getting older, your health is getting worse, you know, like you are senile, you don't know what you're saying.

While Doris and Alma found this abuse both offensive and tiresome, this episode might be taken as an example of the toleration or accommodation of discrimination. Doris reports seeking the support of the warden (and the housing association's head office) who shrugs off her complaint, highlighting the way that everyday racism is often denied or trivialised by those whose lives are not troubled by it (Essed 1991). As such, an alternative reading is that this account reveals the disempowered situation these women are in, compounded by a lack of support and recognition by those with the authority to take action. Poor understanding on the part of the housing association regarding the impact and effect of everyday discrimination means that it is allowed to pass unchallenged.

Public services

The focus groups in Leeds discussed problems with public transport, and buses in particular. The Irish group talked about bus drivers cracking Irish jokes and mimicking their accents. However, they agreed that drivers were not as offensive as they used to be, putting this down partly to the fact that 'the Asian community used to complain so much'.

When the African/Caribbean group talked of buses driving off when they saw older people coming they were asked about race:

Are these white bus drivers?

Yes, there is hardly any black, so the majority is white.

But you think they are making that decision because you are an older person not just because ...?

Well, they have been doing it for yonks. It ain't just happening, been doing it a long time.

So the question of whether the drivers' behaviour was a result of the respondents' age or their race is left open here, highlighting the difficulties associated with articulating ambiguous incidents where uncertainty exists over the motives of others. It is clear from this exchange that the issue to hand is the disrespect shown by the bus drivers and the disruption and inconvenience it causes to the respondents. However, it also illustrates the challenges associated with gathering evidence of discrimination and the problems arising when seeking to label incidents in ways that may not reflect how people interpret everyday events such as these.

Travelling

A question about age discrimination in their countries of origin elicited mixed responses. One user of the day centre in Leeds spoke of her experiences in Barbados:

> *I wouldn't like to go back home now on my own to live. The younger people has adopted I am sorry to say, but the English style, the Western style, and nobody takes much interest of you because you are of older generation. You do not get the respect from them, like what we were brought up to do with older people. So I wouldn't think of going back home.*

An interesting aspect to this comment is that it frames generational relations in cultural terms. This participant had expected Barbados to be how she remembered it, and was shocked by what she found on visiting it most recently.

The experience of travelling can itself generate instances of age discrimination, but both accounts of this that were put forward in the focus groups, were positive. Here is the example provided by Mrs Stuart:

> *I was waiting in a chair and [...] this white lad came up to me and he says 'Where are you going?' and I tell him, 'I am being transferred to go on further.' He said, 'Have you got someone to take you to the plane?' I said, 'No, I can get there myself.' He says, 'No you can't.' So I says, 'Yes I can' [laughs]. So he says, 'You stay here until I come back. I have to take that man' – which was a white gentleman as well – 'right out to the plane. I'll take you as well.' He says, 'But in future, whenever you come*

back to this airport, how regular do you travel?' I says, 'Every year.' He says, 'When you come back here, you tell them you want someone to wheel you out to the plane. It is too far for you to walk on your own, it is really far.' And I thought that was very good and I thought, well in future, I will do that.

Some people may have been offended by the presumptuousness of the airport worker. Seemingly he saw Mrs Stuart waiting and decided that she needed to be wheeled out to the plane. Despite her attempts to refuse, she was, it would appear, charmed and perhaps relieved when he insisted that she should comply. It is clearly an example of age discrimination (possibly linked to signs of physical impairment), but one which in some situations is humiliating and unwanted and in others very welcome and appreciated. As such, it is an exchange that underlines the situated quality of discrimination, the outcome on this occasion proves relatively benign but the broader issue of assuming physical impairment due to age is by no means always so.

DISCUSSION

These two projects used one-off discussion groups to gain an insight into the experience of discrimination. Despite constraints on time and numbers, a diverse and layered narrative on ageing and discrimination was offered by participants. The data gathered cover experiences stretching back over five decades, reach across many aspects of daily life and touch upon the very different levels that discrimination operates. The research shows what 'appears' as discrimination for people who have faced it continuously for a large portion of their lives, and underlines their capacity to interpret and articulate new experiences in light of this. The group situation allowed participants and facilitators alike an opportunity to compare and reflect on their experiences and to air shared understandings.

A significant element of the Bradford discussions was the temporal dimension to discrimination emphasised by the participants. Much of what is related here illustrates the way discrimination punctuates people's lives creating successive setbacks and obstacles. It is interesting to set these accounts against the current backdrop of policy and anti-discrimination legislation that largely fails to acknowledge or recognise the cumulative quality of discrimination. This context underlines the importance of heeding the experiences of those who are subject to discrimination rather than focusing exclusively upon the actions of those who discriminate.

The Bradford project illustrates the multiple set-backs faced by many migrants and how different forms of discrimination are woven into this. Such a picture supports a biographical perspective on discrimination and emphasises the linkages between different phases in a person's life in understanding how disadvantage can build up over time (Gunnarsson 2002). O'Rand (1996) has argued that the influence of earlier experiences in life 'anchor diverse trajectories in old age'. For instance, disadvantage and the effects of discrimination are amplified over time for many migrants. This was outlined by the participants who related the way work, health and housing histories combine to create hardship and privation in old age. O'Rand also highlights the role of institutions in both maintaining and compounding inequalities via the uneven distribution of 'precious' resources, a process well illustrated by some of the accounts gathered here, for instance regarding access to welfare benefits and rights of residence.

Discussion for the Leeds project tended to focus on present-day experience. Accounts offered by participants illustrate the interweaving of different forms of discrimination and the uncertainty sometimes associated with interpreting and labelling particular events. Such uncertainty serves to underline the challenges inherent in dealing with intersecting forms of discrimination and raises questions of how important or useful it is to separate out different forms of discrimination in order to challenge them. For instance, when a bus driver pulls away just as someone approaches, is the salient question here whether such actions are driven by racism or ageism, or rather what effect they have?

The focus on the micropolitics of everyday encounters also signals the value of letting firsthand experience inform understandings of discrimination. While media representations of race relations and immigration have concentrated on 'flashpoints' such as riots and uprisings including clashes with the British National Party (Richmond 1994), discussion with older migrants has underlined the on-going daily pressures of discrimination. In many respects this point goes to the heart of the issue of understanding 'everyday discrimination' (Essed 1991). It is the often insidious and largely overlooked patterns of day to day interaction that are emphasised by participants as most significant to their lives rather than the headline-grabbing turbulence caused when tensions over-spill. To what extent age influences this choice of emphasis is difficult to gauge but clearly for many participants there is a different story to be told from that which concerns the media or policy-makers.

Older people from minority ethnic groups are experienced in coping with discrimination, and our research has produced evidence to suggest that this may equip some to recognise if not cope with age discrimination, perhaps more readily than other older people. However, some indicated feeling less disadvantaged now than they did earlier in life when challenged by racial discrimination and, as a result, they questioned whether age discrimination is of any real consequence by comparison. Does this imply they had learnt how to tolerate prejudice? For example, none of the participants in Leeds said they were offended by ageist birthday cards. On the contrary, some were inclined to collaborate with the jokes by interpreting them as only applying to others.

But the notion of toleration or accommodation of discrimination has been questioned here, not least in that it appears to over-simplify what has been shown to be a complex issue. The term 'tolerance' seems to imply a degree of passive acceptance, but it is important not to confuse the disempowered situation of many older migrants with one of passivity. The picture drawn by respondents for both projects is one of repeated, on-going and persistent discrimination experienced on a day to day basis, even in the most fleeting of social encounters. What would it mean to continuously challenge and resist this level of prejudice? And how easy would that challenge be when so much 'everyday' discrimination is downplayed or discounted by others?

CONCLUSION

Our research has highlighted the importance of family and of the networks that develop between migrants. It is clear that migrant communities in Bradford and Leeds share a history of arduous work, poor pay, restricted access to healthcare and welfare benefits and poor housing, but the effect upon their lives is often buffered by strong family and community ties. It seems reasonable to conclude that people whose lives have been dominated by poverty approach later life with fewer expectations than those who have been – and who remain – more secure financially. Contrasts exist between those for whom advantages have accumulated over time and those who have seen earlier disadvantage compounded as they age. As this study has made clear, discrimination, in many forms, plays a crucial role in this process.

Most importantly, both projects illustrate the complexities of living with different and overlapping forms of discrimination. Debates on intersectionality have emphasised how anti-discrimination initiatives can ignore certain standpoints (Crenshaw 1989, 1994) and this was illustrated by the RoAD project itself, where initial consultation with a network of forums of older people led to only rare contact with black and minority ethnic individuals. Alongside this, the projects have revealed that reports of firsthand experiences show a very different emphasis on the experience of discrimination to that highlighted by the media and both local and national government. It is difficult to escape the conclusion that any attempt to both define and understand multiple discrimination should begin with the participation of those who are subject to it and who may offer a unique brand of expertise as a result.

Acknowledgement

We would like to acknowledge the advice and encouragement of Myfanwy Franks and Mary Maynard who contributed a paper to the seminar on Age-Old Prejudices.

REFERENCES

Ahmad, W. (2002) Family obligations and social change among Asian communities, in Ahmad, W. and Atkin, K. (eds) *'Race' and Community Care*, Buckingham: Open University Press.

Amin, A. (2002) Ethnicity and the multi-cultural city: living with diversity, *Environment and Planning A*, 34(6), 959–80.

Crenshaw, K.W. (1989) Demarginalising the intersections of race and sex, University of Chicago Legal Forum, cited in Fredman, S. (2005) Double trouble: discrimination and EU law, *European Anti-Discrimination Law Review*, 2, 13–18.

Crenshaw, K.W. (1994) Mapping the margins: intersectionality, identity politics, and violence against women of color, in Fineman, M.A. and Mykitiuk, R. (eds) *The Public Nature of Private Violence*, New York: Routledge, pp. 93–118. http://www.hsph.harvard.edu/ Organizations/healthnet/WoC/feminisms/crenshaw.html

Essed, P. (1991) *Understanding Everyday Racism: An Interdisciplinary Theory*, London: Sage.

Gunnarsson, E. (2002) The vulnerable life course: poverty and social assistance among middle-aged and older women, *Ageing and Society*, 22, 709–28.

Hussain, Y. and Bagguley, P. (2005) Citizenship, ethnicity and identity: British Pakistanis after the 2001 'Riots', *Sociology*, 39(3), 407–25.

Kundnani, A. (2001) From Oldham to Bradford: the violence of the violated, *Race and Class*, 43(2), 105–31.

McKibbin, R. (2006) *A Total Transformation*, Commission for Racial Equality, http://www.cre.gov.uk/anthology_28.html.

O'Rand, A. (1996) The precious and the precocious: understanding cumulative disadvantage and cumulative advantage over the life course, *The Gerontologist*, 36(2), 230–38.

Platt, L. (2007) The intergenerational social mobility of minority ethnic groups, *Sociology*, 39(3), 445–61.

Popoviciu, L. and Mac an Ghaill, M. (2004) Racisms, ethnicities and British nation-making, in Devine, F. and Waters, M. (eds) *Social Inequalities in Comparative Perspective*, Oxford: Blackwell.

Richmond, A.H. (1994) *Global Apartheid: Refugees, Racism, and the New World Order*, Oxford: Oxford University Press.

Sharpe, P. (2001) *Women, Gender and Labour Migration: Historical and Global Perspectives*, London: Routledge.

Shaw, A. (2000) *Kinship and Continuity: Pakistani Families in Britain*, London: Routledge.

Sin, C.II. (2005) Experiencing racism: reflections on the practice of research with minority ethnic older people in Britain, *International Journal of Research Methodology*, 8(2), 101–15

Sly, F. (1994) Ethnic groups and the labour market, *Employment Gazette*, May, 147–59.

Summerfield, C. and Babb, P. (2003) *Social Trends, No. 33*, London: HMSO.

Valentine, G. and McDonald, I. (2004) *Understanding Prejudice: Attitudes Towards Minorities*, Stonewall, http://www.stonewall. org. uk/documents/Understanding_Prejudice.pdf

Webster, C. (2003) Race, space and fear: imagined geographies of racism, crime, violence and disorder in Northern England, *Capital and Class*, 80, 95–122.

3

THE SAME HAIRDO

The production of the stereotyped image
of the older woman

ANTHEA SYMONDS AND CAROLINE HOLLAND

INTRODUCTION

I found that Tuesdays were the days to avoid going to the hairdresser's because it's pension day. Pensioners' days are the ones to avoid. Everyone comes out with the same hairdo. White hair that looks a bit like balls of white cotton wool all tight curls with a back brush. White hair all curled up, I went once and came out like that. (Moira,[1] a RoAD diarist)

This chapter considers how the hairstyles of older women are selected and produced. Is there age discrimination in the hairdressing services that they are offered and receive? If there is, is this of any importance? Compared to issues such as access to health services or the vulnerability of people living in care homes, hairdressing may seem a trivial issue. Yet it exemplifies very well the complexity of age discrimination in the everyday, taken-for-granted experience of older people, where there is little clarity about ageist intentions or discriminatory outcomes.

In particular we discuss the attitudes and aspirations of women who took part in a small study of hair and hairdressing within the RoAD project. Initially a number of older people were invited to keep diaries recording experiences as older people and one, Moira, quoted above, drew our attention to her frustration in being unable to find a hairdresser who would offer her a style that she felt would suit her. Her comments were so persuasive that we decided to delve deeper into the phenomenon of 'the pensioner's hairdo' and what it might signify.

---

[1] All names are pseudonyms.

Hair as a social symbol

Hairstyles are important cultural artefacts 'because they are simultaneously public (visible to everyone), personal (biologically linked to the body), and highly malleable to suit cultural and personal preferences' (Weitz 2001, also citing Firth 1973, and Synott 1987). Like clothing and makeup, the hairstyle provides information about age as well as social class, ethnicity, sexual orientation and gender, and it can convey symbolism both of individuality and of group identity (Gimlin 1996; Perutz 1970).

Synott (1993) argues that hair is a cross-cultural sign but, in Western cultures especially, it denotes the binary divisions by which society can be interpreted and managed: old/young, male/female, conservative/radical, heterosexual/homosexual and black/white. Arguably these concepts help people to make sense of everyday life and interpret power relations in society. As we look around, we use our own cultural knowledge and assumptions as well as our own biographical context, as the lens through which we can judge other people's hairstyles. Where we recognise normative frameworks regarding appearance, we can interpret a person's choice of hairstyle accordingly.

For the young, hairstyles have historically been a fundamental badge of belonging to youth subcultures, which sometimes pose a 'threat' or challenge to dominant social forces (Hebdige 1979). Many schools in the UK, for example, continue to implement rules on acceptable hairstyles and exclude students who do not conform. The concept of an 'appropriate hairstyle' – for school or for work – implies the 'inappropriate hairstyle' and there are many examples of people being required to cut their hair shorter, grow it longer, or otherwise re-style it to move from 'deviance' to institutional acceptability.

In terms of gender, appropriate hairstyles have historically been embedded in definitions of acceptable sexuality. For most of the nineteenth and early twentieth century, long hair on men was associated with an 'arty' lifestyle and possible homosexuality, as personified by Oscar Wilde. On women, however, long hair was a sign of sexual attractiveness and femininity, while short hair was associated with the intellectual 'blue stocking' and lesbianism, as personified by Radclyffe Hall. Men who chose to grow their hair long and women who cut their hair short therefore were seen to be making a statement about themselves, whether the intent was political or a matter of fashion. Similarly, the explosion of the hippie culture in the 1960s and 1970s associated long hair on men with political dissent and more specifically with opposition to the Vietnam War: long hair was 'read' as a refusal to become part of an army machine and its inevitable demand for conformity to the different set of values symbolised by very short hair.

What then are we to make of the 'pensioner's hairdo' and what does it tell us about acceptability, deviance, inclusion, and discriminatory practice in later life? Is this a style that older women and others consider to be 'appropriate', and if so what does it say about the permitted image of the older woman?

Hair and the older woman

Beyond consideration of the hair itself, the physical body of a person is the part of them that is subject to the immediate gaze of others. There are arguments that this has different implications for women and men. For example the feminist art historian Griselda Pollock (2001) has argued that the increasing sexualisation of the female body in the visual arts from the early nineteenth century onwards encapsulated the social and gender hierarchy of male body (clothed) viewing female body (naked). Discussing ageing, Susan Sontag (1972) forcefully stated the double standard which attaches to the outward manifestations of ageing: for women, their face and whole presented appearance is a symbol not of what they are 'really like' but of how they wish to be perceived, especially (for heterosexual women) by the male gaze. In later life many older women live in a world dominated by other women and a pervasive down-playing of their sexuality. Nevertheless this gendered understanding of personal appearance together with the normative connection between youth and sexual attractiveness presents older women with challenges about how they present themselves to others.

The gendered 'double standard' of ageing was, until recently, clearly illustrated in the appearance of grey hair. For women, grey had connotations of ageing which meant loss of sexual attractiveness and desirability. For men, it was a sign of sophistication and sexual maturity. Synott notes that in the 1970s young men ambitious for promotion were frequently encouraged to 'look more distinguished by greying their sideburns' (Synott 1993: 110). With the increasing emphasis on youth in the labour market and in information technology especially, this has now changed and men, like women, are urged by TV adverts to 'wash away the grey'. But there remains a difference in motivation: for men it is seen as a pragmatic step in order to secure a job or success at work but, for women, grey hair somehow contradicts their essential value as desirable. One exception is among 'women seeking women' adverts in the press, where the possession of grey hair has sometimes been projected as an attractive feature, symbolising sophistication and worldly experience. But in general, grey hair on a woman crosses two binary systems: old/young and male/female to produce one of the least desirable personas in Western society – an old woman. Even health scares do not deter women from colouring their hair, with women reportedly stating that 'they were rather die than not dye' (Synott 1993: 110). But colouring carries other risks; of being seen to have 'golliwog black hair' (Fairhurst 1998: 264) or of joining the dreaded 'blue rinse brigade'. The process known as streaks or highlights is the way of getting 'youth in a bottle' according to *Good Housekeeping* magazine.

Eileen Fairhurst (1998) poses two alternatives facing older women: 'growing old gracefully' or 'mutton dressed as lamb'. In her study of attitudes to ageing she reports that men also expressed fears about ageing but these were associated with an ability to be active, not sexually attractive. She reports that the phrase 'mutton dressed as lamb', implying a measure of deception, of age 'passing' as youth, was used frequently by the women she interviewed. The challenge for women as they age is to negotiate a workable compromise between a risible attempt at denying age and a socially dangerous strategy of 'letting oneself go', perhaps signalling vulnerability.

The biological changes that accompany ageing include effects on the hair – drying, greying, thinning – that in the absence of treatments, produce an aged appearance. The management of ageing hair is therefore subject to specific advice about how to maintain an appearance of vigour. For example a recent feature in *Good Housekeeping* magazine entitled 'How a haircut can take years off your looks' (April 2006), describes certain 'rules' such as never have long hair after the age of fifty, going 'one shade lighter' as you get older, and a 'fringe is better than botox'. In spite of these cardinal and often repeated 'rules', achieving a hairdo that makes one feel good about oneself is often a challenge. Moira, the RoAD diarist we quoted above, described her dilemma in this way:

> *As you get older your face changes, of course it does. What I want is a hairdo that compliments me, that makes me look right and better. I hate back-combing, I want a hairstyle that looks flattering, not young and silly but right for me as I am. But they don't seem able to see that, they just do your hair as they think it should be for my age.*

THE RoAD STUDY OF HAIRDRESSING

RoAD was an exercise in participative research. Moira is an 87-year-old widow, a member of an older people's forum in a large city. In her diary, she made the following entry:

> *While I was at Sainsbury's I met a lady I knew, and we walked part of the way home together. On the previous day she had been to a local Hairdressing salon, & referring to her appearance, complained to me that elderly ladies are not given the same consideration as young girls. 'I explained how I wanted it done and I still look like a granny' she said. I asked if she had complained. She replied, 'No – what's the use? They don't listen to you.'*

unheard as well as invisible.

> *I personally found the same problem some time ago, & now make a visit every 6 weeks or so to the House of Fraser in the city for a cut, shampoo etc. In between I wash & set it myself. Prices are quite high, & there is no discount for pensioners, but – in common parlance – it makes me feel more 'with it' (It's probably psychological!). (28 June 2005)*

The insights that Moira gives into the experience of older women seeking a satisfactory service prompted us to undertake further research. We discussed hairstyling for older women with various hairdressers working in a wide variety of salons in various locations in South Wales. At the same time we found the following entry in another RoAD diary. Grace, aged 82, described a visit to her local hairdresser in a small but busy town in South Wales:

Went to the hairdressers over lunchtime which is not at all 'posh' but is friendly – the clientele is all elderly, many with walking sticks but there is absolutely no discrimination though the staff are fairly young. (11 March 2005)

This was Sue's Salon[2] and we were able to arrange to spend a day there talking to Sue's other customers. Her salon is converted from the front room of an ordinary terraced house and is flanked by other houses and some small shops. The door from the street opens straight into the salon which has five chairs and mirrors. At the far end are two wash basins with chairs and two upright hair dryers. There are no photographs of models or hairstyles on the walls. There is a table with magazines in the centre, and the cash desk is a small table with a drawer and telephone. There is a row of hooks on the wall for customers to hang their coats. It is not always easy to see when a person comes in through the door, but there is a bell that rings loudly whenever it is opened. The room is bright and recently painted, and the most fitting word to describe it is 'cosy'.

There are two staff in the salon: Sue, the owner, and Kate, her assistant. Sue does all the setting and combing out of hair for the shampoos and sets. Kate does the shampooing, and the blow dries for those customers who do not want a formal shampoo and set. Both answer the phone or, if necessary, ask customers to do so. Kate makes coffee or tea in a 'quiet period' and both women take payment and give change. Only cash is accepted. The shop opens three and a half days a week (Tuesday, Thursday, Friday and Saturday morning), from nine in the morning until two in the afternoon.

We were there on a Friday, traditionally the busiest day of the week for hairdressers and the shop was busy throughout. Both hairdressers kept up a constant conversation and neither stopped for lunch or a coffee break. In the five hours of opening, 25 clients were seen (most hairdressers operate on a ratio of two clients per hour per stylist). There is no formal appointment system and all clients appeared willing to wait their turn. No prices were on display, but they seemed to be familiar with the price and often had the right money ready.

---

[2] This is a pseudonym.

Sue says they cater exclusively for older women and have no male clients. It is relatively cheap and she tries to project the image of a friendly service rather than an up-market salon aspiring to attract a younger and more affluent clientele. Grace, in her interview, joked that there are so many older customers that 'you're falling over the walking sticks and zimmer frames', and the salon does seem similar to the hairdressing rooms we have seen in residential homes. There is a social atmosphere in which everyone is known to everyone else. Sue and Kate are young enough to be the granddaughters of most of the clients.

We talked to fifteen of the clients, ranging in age from 60 to the mid-eighties. A range of topics were covered, including their reasons for going to Sue's salon every week; the importance they place on how their hair looks; their attitudes to colouring; difficulties they might have in doing their own hair; and finally their thoughts on ageing and self-image.

A regular routine

All the women interviewed visit the hairdresser every week. This pattern of regular weekly visits is borne out by conversations with other hairdressers who all reported that older women tend to visit much more often than younger women. They explained that whereas older women tend not to do their own hair between visits, younger women like to wash their hair more often (some every day) and to visit a hairdresser for a cut only once every four to six weeks. This difference is noted by hairdressers at the 'upmarket' end as well as those such as Sue offering a lower cost service. Sue's clients seemed to come at the same time every week and they offered reasons for their pattern of regular visiting:

medical issues re. hair care -

> *I like having my hair done. It's important because when you get older you can't do it yourself. At least I can't now because I have arthritis. I only used to go to the hairdressers to have a perm and set it myself, unless I was going somewhere special – but I don't do it now.* (Freda)

> *I don't bother to do my own hair. I get awful pain in my arms if I reach up.* (Gwen)

32

Others, without invoking a physical inability to manage their hair, said they were 'hopeless' at doing it. In contrast, others said they needed a weekly visit in order to look smart:

I like to look tidy, that's why I come every week. (Connie)

Olive expressed pleasure and reassurance in the weekly routine:

It's nice to have someone doing your hair for you, nice to know it's done regularly. I do it myself in between, but I come every week. (Olive)

The majority of women did not appear to actively choose the style of their hair. They said they preferred to stick to the style they had had for many years, or to leave it to Sue to decide what would be an appropriate style. Olive went on to describe how she has adapted to the changes that she ascribes to physical ageing:

I've had the same style for years, I don't want to change it. I always prefer to have it done on rollers. Trendy hairdressers don't know how, they don't know how to do older people's hair, they don't have a flair for older people. I had a blow dry once and it came straight out. I used to have highlights but I don't bother now as my hair is thinner than it used to be. I think this is due to blood pressure tablets, they slow me down and make me feel tired, but the doctor says that I have to keep taking them. (Olive)

The main requirement for several of the women was that the hairdo should 'last' and not come 'straight out'. Freda for example likes to have it set 'because it will last until next Friday'. If she had it blow dried, she claimed, it wouldn't last. Sue has considerable influence in determining what is needed to ensure that the hairdo lasts, as is evident in Anne's account:

I've always had blow dries but, the last time I was here, I had it rollered because I was going to Prague, and Sue said that a set would give my hair more body and it did. It stayed in for a whole week but I didn't really like it. (Anne)

Chris, at 60 the youngest woman we conversed with, is an exception. She refuses the perms that Sue suggests:

I have a blow dry, but sometimes I have it coloured because it gives my hair body. I've always had fine hair. Here they encourage you to have a perm but I would never have a perm. I don't like hair curly, I prefer it straight. A lot of the older age group still like perms, I think because they always used to be publicised in magazines but now straight hair is in. I remember when all hair was backcombed. You had no choice. (Chris)

In the above descriptions, both Chris and Olive refer to how they have had their hair coloured. Some of the women expressed an aversion to grey hair. Vi, for example, said it 'horrified' her and Hazel thought it was too 'dominating'. Anne said she had it coloured because 'you've got to hold back age for as long as you can'. Resistance to age combines with a loyalty both to the past and to Sue's judgement, as in the following responses:

I like to have it blow dried, I don't like my hair too tight. A blow dry makes you look younger. I always have the same blow dry, but I like it a bit curly. That's how my husband used to like it. He's been dead for 27 years now, but I keep it the same. I like to have a rinse every two months. It makes me look and feel younger. I won't go grey unless the time comes when I can't be bothered. (Connie)

I always have my hair done the same way. Sue knows how I like it. Modern hairstyles don't suit older people. But I hate grey hair, grey ages you. (Rita)

Other women were more accepting of grey hair: it was part of 'growing old gracefully'. Olive pointed out that 'we don't grow young' and Lorraine argued that 'as you get older you are less adventurous'. Freda explained how being smart is more important than resisting age:

I'm having a cut today, then I'll have a perm at the end of March so that it's right for Easter. I like to have my hair set (on rollers), but I'm letting my hair go grey gently and naturally. I don't mind grey hair. The worst thing about getting old is that your bones get older. (Freda)

For most of these women, their main concern was to maintain an appearance that showed they were still in control, that they looked tidy and well groomed. They wanted to achieve this with the minimum of fuss and cost. They relied on Sue, especially those who had difficulty in managing their own hair.

The social role of the salon

For many, the salon had become more than just a place where they went to have their hair done. Rather it was a social world where they felt valued and at ease. Familiarity generated a sense of security and belonging. In contrast to their negative experiences of less age-friendly settings, in this salon they felt comfortable and included.

A number of words and phrases recur in the following quotes. 'Friendly', 'pleasant', 'loyalty' and 'feel good' represent a degree of mutual affection. 'Laugh' and 'chat' and phrases such as 'get together', 'like a social' and 'out of the house' indicate that, for many, the salon has a social function. 'Cheap', 'reasonable' and 'near' remind us that expense and convenience are also critical factors.

I meet a lot of people here. It's like having a get together every week. (Freda)

They always fit me in. My daughters go to Gerson's and Emmanuella's. They're happy there and I'm happy here, although they laugh at me. But I think people are loyal to one hairdresser. (Chris)

They're reasonable, well cheap really. They're very friendly and you don't feel out of place. These modern ones I feel out of place in. (Rita)

They're pleasant and we always have a laugh. It's so friendly. (Hazel)

It's lovely and friendly and I know everyone. It's reasonable and every one is the same age. (Vi)

It's the same crowd every week. I've been coming for years. (Lorraine)

35

It's like a social, we have a chat and it gets you out of the house, that's the main thing. (Margaret)

Everyone's the same age. (Doris)

I like the company, it's friendly and happy. (Sheila)

It's near, it's friendly and it cheers you up. (Peggy)

The atmosphere, you meet people and have a chat. (Betty)

You see the same people every week, it's great. (Gwen)

I come here because they're friendly and I see the same people every week. I need a hairdresser close to where I live, otherwise if the weather is bad my hair do blow out before I get home. This place is convenient. I can get off the bus by the gardens and come here. Then when my hair is finished I can go shopping. (Connie)

I like it because it gets me out of the house, that's the important thing, to go out. (Doris)

I come every Friday. I meet people and have a chat. It makes you feel good when your hair is tidy. (Betty)

'Same', 'always' and 'every' imply regularity and a lack of change, security and the comfort of the familiar. When Vi says the salon is lovely because it's friendly and reasonable, and because she knows everyone and they are all the same age, she is articulating very concisely how these women have chosen to join what they see to be an age-specific 'community'. Similarly, when Chris says her daughters are happy going to Gerson's and Emmanuella's and she is happy going to Sue's, she is expressing an acceptance of this kind of age segregation.

These comments demonstrate the essentially social nature of the service being provided by Sue. Within this friendly, unchanging and unchallenging environment, the women feel included and valued. Stepping outside the salon, they re-emerge into a world where this is not always the case and where the physical appearance of age may have a negative impact on how they are treated. This is what Moira had experienced when she found a salon that did not offer any reductions. In the interview following completion of her diary, she described the following experience:

I went into town and found a hairdresser's that had no reduction and you paid like everyone else. This was better but still not the same. Admittedly I have my hair set in rollers they put you under the hairdryer and there you are. But with young girls they hover round them for hours and I thought they don't leave that young woman for a minute. They are fussing round them until the hair is finished. And I'm paying the same money. I have to stop them back brushing.

What is so revealing about this account is the significance Moira places upon attention, cost and styling. She felt that she was being offered a raw deal: little attention and poor consultation over style, despite paying the same money. And this was the result of her attempt to avoid the cotton-wool hairdo.

Appearance and role models

Just as Eileen Fairhurst had found in her research, many of the women we interviewed in Sue's Salon feared that they might appear as 'mutton dressed as lamb'. At the same time, they did not wish to be seen as 'old women'. This they interpreted both as a state of being and of being defined by others. They had gained an understanding of what 'old' looks like in the middle of the last century. Growing up, as most of them had, in small towns in South Wales, being 'old' was represented by their mothers: women who had reached a stage in their life when they had 'settled down', married with children, having the status of a 'mam', sheltered from the job market and occupying an identifiable domestic role. Family photographs taken at the time show women dressed in ways that they now think of as typical of old women:

When I think of how my mother looked, she was always in an apron with her hair scraped back, no make up, she always seemed old. But I was only thinking the other day, when she was like that she was only in her early fifties, much younger than I am now, but she always seemed old, everyone did, they don't now. (Betty)

The power of the mother–daughter relationship in determining appearance and interpretations of age is powerfully evident in Chris's experience:

I don't look in shops for older people. If I do, my daughters whizz me past, but I still have this notion of 'mutton dressed as lamb'. I think this idea is instilled into us. Now if I try something on that I like and I can see my mother in it, I change my mind. I don't want to look like that. (Chris)

Was age understood differently a generation ago? Is 'being old' dependent upon time, place and culture? Stuart Hall, the cultural theorist, writing about the meaning of being 'black' has argued that 'blackness' is not an innate 'essence' (Hall 1992). Rather, he claims, a black identity can be constructed and reconstructed by people within changing sets of cultural, historical and spatial conditions. Likewise it can be argued that the women we interviewed have an image of 'being old' that is dependent upon time, place and culture. Living in a changed cultural and economic context to that of their mothers, they are attempting to construct an alternative, more positive, identity. But what, and how?

Media representations of youth and age have a strong influence, not only directly on individual women but also on the culture around them. With their own mothers' generation no longer providing attractive role models for ageing, some have turned to the media for clues about what is appropriate. Some of the women in Sue's Salon said they read fashion magazines but were dissatisfied with the range of clothes available to older women in local shops. Many liked watching the 'make over' shows on television, but again remarked on how they always focused on young people. It was clear however that, despite perceiving that older women as a consumer group are not adequately catered for, some did identify with celebrity role models such as soap stars, and were interested in how they managed their appearance. The following comment from Connie is an example of how they look for such guidance in attempting to present a satisfying image of themselves:

I like looking at hairstyles in magazines, but I don't change mine. I like looking at the way celebrities do their hair and dress, especially Gloria Hunniford, but her hair is going thin, but they must have a way of doing it to disguise the fact. (Connie)

The names of television celebrities such as Gloria Hunniford and soap opera characters came up several times in conversation during the course of our day in the salon. Perhaps this is not surprising given that Sue's clients had been meeting there regularly for many years and, presumably, exchanging comments and opinions about these stars of the mass media.

They also exchanged information about local clothing retailers, and the likelihood of finding clothes at the right price and quality, clothes that reflected the kind of image they sought for themselves. Chris, for example, noted that her experience of shopping at Monsoon was 'good', but there were less positive reports from others:

> *I buy clothes in Marks, especially Per Una, Debenham's and JT Morgan. I don't get any trouble with sizes, although Marks can be a bit 'iffy' with sizes. It's because they're paying peanuts in countries for having their clothes made cheap, that's why the clothes are too small.* (Anne)

> *All the decent shops are gone. Marks now only caters for young people.* (Lorraine)

> *The only places for my age that I can afford are Tesco's and Marks. There's not a lot of scope otherwise.* (Doris)

The consumer market, mass media and social policies project a hegemonic view of ageing. However, rather than older people being included in a model of cultural diversity, they are seen to be in a state of decline and needing support and care. A multicultural society is not a multi-age one. The women we spoke to were conscious that in many contexts their age defined them as 'old'. Sue provides them with a comfortable and non-threatening environment in which to socialise whilst having their hair dressed, but she herself is a part of the age-defining mechanism and she is skilled and experienced in providing them with a powerful signifier of age: the 'pensioner's hairdo'. Some of her clients expressed a wish for a less ageing or more personalised appearance whilst also, it would appear, being very conscious of what was regarded as appropriate and dignified for women of their age. Others appeared happy to stick with the uniform appearance offered by Sue. With this, they knew they would be included in their peer group, and identified in the wider society as one of that group.

Within an all-enveloping culture of discrimination by assumption, to what extent can older people construct an alternative identity? Can older women resist the assumptions that are based upon their physical appearance? Some of Sue's clients offered thoughts on getting older and how expectations are changing. Some took the view that 'staying young' or, at least, fending off old age was a personal choice and almost a moral responsibility. Ann for example argued that 'there's no need for people to look old these days' and, drawing upon her own experience, Vi argued that her generation 'wants to stay young':

> They don't want to give up work, they want to stay busy. I think they're going to raise the retirement age – it will be a good thing too. I had to retire when I was only 57 because of an injury through lifting. The consultant said that I couldn't go back to the same job. I had compensation but it's not the same as working. When you're at home all day you're not as organised as you are when you go out to work. People should do their best to stay young. (Vi)

Discrimination by image is powerful and pervasive. The images conveyed by hairdressing salons to the passing public provide clear indications of what kinds of clients are welcome. Photographs displaying possible hairstyles, for example, set standards that attract some and deter others. Although upmarket hairdressing salons may claim to cater for women of all ages, they only use youthful models and assistants to attract customers and to display the different styles. The industry may argue that everyone, older people included, prefer to identify with younger, youthful images. In response, Germaine Greer (2005) describes the prevailing climate as 'gerontophobia'. This she argues is so powerful that many older people themselves 'are in denial'. They actively dissociate themselves from the stereotype of age: 'lonely, ill and poor, with no spending power, no clout, no glamour', and even join in with the stereotyping of the unfortunate 'others'. Some older actresses for example, Greer argues, have gained success by producing unflattering portrayals of women their own age.

The others are expected to retreat to the comforts of salons such as Sue's, tolerating the consequences of the same old cheap hairdo. Betty, another diarist, answered the question 'Are there occasions when you are out and about, for example when you're at the hairdressers, and you feel you're being treated in a certain way because of your age?' with the reply: 'At the hairdressers I go to, if you go Monday, Tuesday or Wednesday then you get it cheaper. So I always go Monday, Tuesday or Wednesday. So they're all pensioners.'

This echoes other research with postmenopausal women in south Wales. One for example commented:

> Obviously my body's older, wrinkles and generally going to seed ... I welcome that actually, it gives you a breather, you can sit back and observe more and I like that.
>
> (Morris and Symonds 2004: 318)

The map of 'how to grow old' was clear for women of Betty's mother's generation. It was about settling down, raising children and keeping the house. Listening to the women in Sue's Salon, it would seem that a new map offering different routes and destinations needs to be drawn up. Appearance is an important sign of the route being chosen by individuals, but how free are individuals to choose between different images?

CONCLUSION

Bourdieu and Wacquare (1992: 74) defined 'socially constituted agoraphobia' as people voluntarily excluding themselves from a range of public activities from which they are already structurally excluded. Several women we met in Sue's Salon remarked on the feeling of 'not belonging' when in upmarket salons. They felt uncomfortable when entering them and had the impression that the staff did not want them as customers. This was how Moira felt when she decided to try the salon in town, leaving her feeling she had had a raw deal in terms of attention and styling. Such experiences perhaps illustrate the road to agoraphobia. When a person feels unwelcome as s/he crosses the threshold of commercial premises this is an active achievement on the part of that establishment. It is the result of a host of practices sometimes, as Moira's experience illustrates, entirely unremarkable and embedded in the working routines of the staff. The question is why there is such a powerful investment in marking out settings such as hairdressers in this way. We might also question how such practices are learned and passed on as an integral feature of working in the industry.

In producing the stereotyped image of the older woman, represented so graphically in 'the pensioner's hairdo', the salon itself plays a significant role. Older women are repeatedly reminded that they do not 'fit' the image of the high class salon. Hairdressers use photographs in advertisements in the local media, in the magazines strewn about their premises, in their windows and on the walls of their salons not only to display different styles but to attract the attention of different categories of clientele. Most of these photographs are of young models displaying fashionable hairstyles. Advertisers have generally defended this practice on the grounds that older people prefer to relate to younger images rather than older ones. In this way, the physical and material environment is made to collude with the discriminatory and differentiating practices employed by the staff and, at a wider level, upheld by the industry.

The sense of 'belonging' or 'fitting' is crucial both within the environment of the hair salon and in the choices available to many older people. While Sue's Salon offered a limited choice of styles, it provided a secure and inclusive environment in which older customers did not feel disrespected, unappreciated, or in some way lacking in interest to the hairstylist. This is what they had found, or suspected, in more 'up-market' businesses aimed at a younger clientele. The strong sense of appropriateness in hairstyle ('neat', 'lasting', and familiar) was accompanied by a sense of appropriateness of place: at Sue's the women were comfortable, while in the other salons they felt 'out of place'. The repertoire of appropriateness here is a major factor in the (re)creation of self image and self-identity (see Chapter 4). By an iterative process of doing age-appropriate behaviour (being in the right place, choosing the right hairdo) were these customers colluding with engrained age discrimination, or exercising their right as consumers to choose what they liked?

McFarquar and Lowis (2000) provide evidence that the self-esteem of women is raised when they have their hair done. In palliative day care, hairdressing is one of the most important in a range of therapies available (Higginson *et al.* 2000), and it is an almost obligatory service for women in residential and nursing homes and in day care centres. Hairdressing is viewed as on a par with chiropody as a social/health service for older women, and contributes to self-confidence for many. Seen as an essential component of the beauty and fashion world for young women, by contrast hairdressing appears to take on qualities associated with social care as a service for older women. The emphasis on tidiness and functionality in the hairdos chosen by Sue's customers, underlines the customers' need to maintain an outward appearance of competence and control. Self-expression and choice came very much second to these considerations.

The experience of being old, female and poor is not the same as being old, female and wealthy, and one could argue that the pensioner's hairdo is a badge of class as well of age. Substitute the designation of old with young or female with male and of course a different picture of social power emerges, and the dominant factor of wealth remains a key to the unpicking of discriminatory practices. Nevertheless this investigation into hairdressing for older women suggests something of the extent to which older people – and older women in particular – must struggle against an almost overwhelming tide of negativity about their bodies and prejudice about their role in society. Getting a hairdo is just one example of where the personal and the political collide, as the aesthetics of taste meet the practices of discrimination.

REFERENCES

Bourdieu, P. and Wacquare, L. (1992) *Invitation to Reflexive Sociology*, Cambridge: Polity Press.

Fairhurst, E. (1998) 'Growing old gracefully' as opposed to 'mutton dressed as lamb', in Nettleton, S. and Watson, J. (eds), *The Body in Everyday Life,* London: Routledge.

Firth, R. (1973) *Symbols: Public and Private*, Ithaca, NY: Cornell University Press.

Gimlin, D. (1996) Pamela's place: power and negotiation in the hair salon, *Gender and Society*, 10(5), 505–26.

Greer, G. (2005) For whom the bells toll, *Society Guardian,* 14 September.

Hall, S. (1992) What is this 'black' in black popular culture?, in Dent, G. (ed.), *Black Popular Culture,* Seattle: Bay Press.

Hebdige, D. (1979) *Subculture: the Meaning of Style,* London: Methuen.

Higginson, I., Hearn, J. and Myers, K. (2000) Palliative day care: what do services do? *Palliative Medicine,* 14, 277–86.

McFarquar, C. and Lowis M. (2000) The effect of hairdressing on the self-esteem of men and women, *Mankind Quarterly,* 41(2), 181–92.

Morris, M. and Symonds, A. (2004) 'We've been trained to put up with it': real women and the menopause, *Critical Public Health,* 14(3), 311–23.

Perutz, K. (1970) *Beyond the Looking Glass: Life in the Beauty Culture,* New York: Penguin.

Pollock, G. (2001) Painting, feminism and history, in Gaiger, J. and Wood, P. (eds), *Art of the Twentieth Century,* New York: Yale University Press.

Sontag, S. (1972) The double standard of ageing, *Saturday Review,* 23, 29–38.

Synott, A. (1987) Shame and glory: a sociology of hair, *British Journal of Sociology,* 38, 381–483.

Synott, A. (1993) *The Body Social: Symbolism, Self and Society.* London: Routledge.

Weitz, R. (2001) Women and their hair: seeking power through resistance and accommodation, *Gender and Society,* 15(5), 667–86.

4

INTERSECTIONS OF AGEING AND SEXUALITY
Accounts from older people

RICHARD WARD, REBECCA JONES, JONATHAN HUGHES, NICOLA HUMBERSTONE AND ROSALIND PEARSON

INTRODUCTION

This chapter draws on the findings of a small-scale study that explored how age discrimination relates to sexuality in later life. Contributions to RoAD from older people across the UK indicated that few considered sexuality to be either an appropriate or relevant topic for discussion when asked to relate experiences of age discrimination. This was surprising when stereotyped notions of sexuality in old age appear so commonplace. Such a striking omission suggests that sexuality is disconnected from the ways many people think and talk about ageism and age discrimination. It may even imply that influential narratives of ageing sexuality have the effect of disconnecting older people from their sexualities. In light of this, we decided to undertake a study using interviews to gather accounts from a sexually diverse group of older men and women. The primary concern being with discrimination: how it is expressed and enacted, how it relates to age and sexual identities, and the impact it has on older people.

Sexuality in gerontology

So often is it pointed out that common understandings of ageing and later life overlook sexuality that it has become a cliché of social gerontology. However, moves to sexualise an understanding of ageing have tended to unfold within narrow parameters. In particular the sexual norm is often assumed to be that of heterosexual married intercourse. This ignores the broad spectrum of sexualities. Understandings of ageing sexuality also tend to ignore the shifting ways that such sexualities are represented. Both these factors mean that the perspectives and experiences of many older people across this spectrum are absent from discussion. This is a persistent omission that has shaped gerontological discourses on ageing and identity. Consequently, little thought has been given to the relations of power that imbue sexual differences in old age. In addition, the reactions of older people to these attempts to pin down sexuality are also overlooked.

While heterosexual elders might be considered the focus of mainstream gerontology, their sexual orientation is rarely acknowledged, let alone analysed. Historically, a powerful assumption has been that older people become 'non-sexual'. Even where this is questioned, certain assumptions (such as 'old equals straight') remain characteristic of much existing discussion of later life sexuality (Gott 2005), a practice that has 'heterosexualised' old age. Hegemonic forms of heterosexuality thereby frame the depiction of later life across varied contexts and settings (Cronin 2006; Ward *et al.* 2005). These depictions imply the heterosexual norm of penis–vagina sexual intercourse (within a stable relationship typified by marriage) is the only appropriate expression of sexuality throughout the adult life course. The studies that exist of sexual dissidence in later life are rarely referenced in the 'mainstream' literature on older people and sexuality. Research about older lesbian, gay, bisexual and transgendered people often ends up in a specialist ghetto. This means that research that considers the standpoints of a diverse range of participants is scarce, and the consequent potential for recognising sexual diversity in later life is generally overlooked. The absence from the debate of older peoples' voices on sexuality makes it difficult to know whether dominant narratives that attempt to prescribe their sexualities are accepted or resisted.

Ageing/Sexuality/Gender

Much evidence has been gathered to suggest that ageing is an intrinsically gendered social process (e.g. Arber and Ginn 1995; Arber *et al.* 2003; Calasanti and Slevin 2001). Correspondingly, intersections of sexism and ageism, it has been argued, distinguish the experience of older women from that of older men. Women face a 'double standard' as they age, premised upon the presupposition of sexual disparity. While men retain their status, at least for as long as they can perform sexually, women are subject to a process of sexual

46

disqualification (Sontag 1979). Women face what has been described as double or multiple ageing, and are 'struck' by age far earlier than men (Woodward 1999; Gullette 1997). The ageism women face has been interpreted as a form of sexism (Macdonald and Rich 1983); the 'loathing and stereotyping' of older women being distinct from either the 'adultism' faced by younger people or the ageism experienced by men (Copper 1988).

Coupled with the cult of youth, age discrimination has also long been attributed to gay male networks (Schaffer 1972; Wahler and Gabbay 1997; Hajek and Giles 2002; Heaphy *et al.* 2003, 2004). Jones and Pugh (2005) have emphasised how the commercial gay scene, characterised by displays of wealth and spending power, tends to exclude older people. The standpoint and experiences of older heterosexual men seem largely absent from attempts to make sense of the intersections of ageing, sexuality and gender. How age discrimination might affect the status or privileges that (heterosexual) men maintain in later life remains largely unexplored. Little effort has been made to establish whether age discrimination presents problems for them as they age and if so, what form it might take.

However, such disparities are never static. Historically, the prevailing assumption has been that eventually men lose the ability to demonstrate their (heterosexual) masculinity by engaging in penetrative sex. When this happened their status as 'real' men was brought into question. This process was considered more or less natural, with men encouraged to accept the inevitable, with good grace and resignation. Subsequently, this advice has been reversed with men increasingly encouraged to maintain 'active' sex lives on the 'use it or lose it' principle (Marshall and Katz 2002; Katz and Marshall 2003). In this changed circumstance, not to remain sexually active becomes a dereliction of male duty and a 'giving in' to ageing. This narrative of active sexuality has been connected even more strongly to heterosexual intercourse by the introduction of Viagra (and other pharmaceutical products) alongside claims that the erections men need to continue 'proper' sex lives are restorable. Never has the need to 'perform' been so openly discussed. This discussion and the development of the concept of erectile dysfunction (ED) mean that heterosexual masculinity has never before been subject to so much intervention and regulation (Marshall 2006; Potts 2000).

THE SEXUALITY AND AGE DISCRIMINATION STUDY

Heterosexual men and women, lesbians and gay men were interviewed for the study[1] using a standardised semi-structured interview schedule.[2] Altogether, 27 older people took part, aged between 55 and 87 years. Five researchers collaborated on the project and were 'matched' as far as possible with interviewees in terms of sexual identity to facilitate open discussion. Inevitably perhaps, such matching proved only approximate as the interviews opened up a diversity of attitudes and practices which were, sometimes, difficult to typify just using the terms gay and straight.

The researchers used existing contacts and networks to recruit interviewees. These included campaigning groups and the mailing list for the RoAD project. Word of mouth and snowballing methods were also employed. This recruitment method made obtaining access to interviewees relatively straightforward and we were able to reach our target number of respondents within a tight timeframe. This is of course an important issue when researching topics affecting marginalised groups. However, it also meant that the people we interviewed tended to be 'activists' to a greater or lesser degree. The people recruited through the RoAD mailing list had already expressed an interest in age discrimination. Most of the lesbians who took part were involved in feminist and lesbian political networks. Some of the heterosexual women and gay men were involved in campaigns around health and care issues and most were in contact with campaigning organisations such as the Growing Old Disgracefully network and Polari. The practice of recruiting interviewees through different networks also raises the possibility that those prepared to discuss their sexuality in this research context might also include individuals more likely to challenge some of the pervasive assumptions that surround ageing and sexuality.

---

[1] We had hoped to also interview bisexual older people but were not able to recruit any within the timescale of the project.
[2] A number of additional questions, specifically relating to the gay and lesbian communities were added for gay and lesbian interviewees.

Most also had a connection to the project or the interviewers. For some it was a connection to The Open University, where the RoAD project was undertaken – many of the heterosexual men turned out to be former OU students. The heterosexual women and one of the lesbians had participated in previous research undertaken by one of the interviewers on a related topic (Jones 2002, 2006). The other lesbians were connected to two of the interviewers through political networks. Some of the gay men had some sort of personal connection to their interviewer (some only 'a friend of a friend'); others had Polari as an intermediary. These personal connections may have contributed to some degree of trust, enabling the frank discussion of potentially sensitive issues that occurred. They are also, of course, not uncommon in research of all types. It would be interesting to know what proportion of respondents in other studies have this sort of loose connection to researchers and organisations.

Interviews were undertaken throughout the UK, but mainly in London and south-east England. The interviews were transcribed in full and exchanged with the other researchers for coding and analysis.

Profiles of the participants

The five heterosexual women were aged between 67 and 81 years. They lived in the south-east of England and in East Anglia. All lived independently; one in sheltered housing and the others in owned or rented property. None received official home care services but several had informal arrangements for help with particular tasks. All were white British; one described herself as a secular Jew. Apart from one still married woman, all had experienced the death of at least one long-term partner. Two were in ongoing sexual relationships; two wished to be. One had been disabled all her life.

The seven heterosexual men ranged in age from 55 to 87 years. They lived in different parts of England, and had diverse working histories. One was still in paid employment at the time of interview. Two were married; the others were divorced, widowed or lived alone. All the men were white British. Many had some form of chronic illness or disability including diabetes, prostate cancer and arthritis. All but one of the men had adult children. The majority were in some form of relationship (typically marriage).

Most of the eight lesbians who participated in the project were active in both feminist and lesbian politics. All but one belonged to groups for older lesbians or older women. They were aged between 63 and 76. One used a wheelchair; another had restricted mobility. They had diverse work histories. One was married before coming out as a lesbian. All but one lived alone; the majority owned their own homes. One lived in an adapted council flat. Two were friends who requested a joint interview. All but one (who lived in a small village in a rural area) lived in or near London.

The seven gay men ranged in age from 59 to 81 years. All were white British with one describing himself as part Philippino; another described his ethnicity as 'gay'. One man was a secular Jew. All lived in London or south east England. All but one were single and lived alone, mainly in privately owned housing, with one in sheltered housing. One had been married with children before coming out as gay. Two men were recently bereaved. Two were in remission from prostate cancer, two reported heart problems, and one had diabetes. Four reported no health problems. Most were involved in groups for gay men and lesbians. One man described himself as a 'tranny' (transvestite) and was an active member of the trans community.

The side-by-side comparison of a sexually diverse group of men and women in this study is unusual and we discuss some of the effects of this research design later in this chapter. Initially we turn to what the participants said about their experiences of age discrimination in relation to sexuality. We discuss this under five main headings: becoming asexual; dating; image and appearance; invisibility; and identity, networks and support.

Becoming asexual?

All groups, men and women, heterosexual and gay, noted in a general sense the 'de-sexing' of old age. Talking of her family, one woman commented:

They don't expect you to want to have a partnership, they don't expect you to want to have a loving relationship, you're just grandma who comes in handy for looking after the kids every now and then and really needs to be looked after a little bit, I think. HW1(73)[3]

In other words, many identities associated with later life are constrained by pressure not to be open regarding sexual feelings or desires, particularly in the context of intergenerational relationships. A number of men also reflected upon encounters with younger people and the impression that a sexualised identity was considered incompatible with later life.

Sometimes yeh, it makes you feel bad when you see people who are younger, the fact of me being a sexual being wouldn't enter their heads. HM1(68)

Because what I'm getting from the gay community is that you are not as sexually attractive when you are older but you'll be a wonderful mentor and supporter and giver but you are not sexually attractive. GM1(59)

The assumption that later life inevitably implies becoming non-sexual was found in some of the accounts of the older (heterosexual) men. In exploring the sexual histories of these men, it became apparent that some go along with the narrative that ageing implies a disconnection from sexuality.

I don't think of sex now, of sexual relationships at all now. HM6(80)

It is worth noting that such comments came from men who did not feel that sexuality was the basis of age discrimination. One interpretation of this might be that it is difficult to perceive discrimination in something that is considered 'natural'.

While the de-sexing of later life forms part of the process by which older people are pressured to conform, this has specific implications for the invisibility of older lesbians and gay men. One woman spoke of how ageist assumptions had veiled her lesbian relationship in the eyes of others:

---

[3] Coding for quotes: HM = heterosexual man, HW = heterosexual woman, L = lesbian, GM = gay man. Each group of interviewees were numbered sequentially i.e. HM1 through 7. The age of each respondent is given in brackets. Occasionally we have used pseudonyms.

For example, if you are going with your partner to stay in a country B&B or something, there used to be that slight [intake of breath] when you turn up and they think they've made a mistake and given you a double bed and [flustered] and say oh, oh and you say no, it's perfectly alright. There doesn't seem to be that any more and I presume that's because two old ladies in the bed together, there's no way they're going to get up to no good. [laughs] L6(63)

Similarly, another commented that when she formed a new relationship in later life, she felt most people assumed they were just friends. She described a routine of kissing her partner goodbye at the bus station:

They just think [...] 'Oh, there's one old lady saying goodbye to her friend.' Now two elderly ladies, they probably wouldn't be kissing quite like that! L8(74)

There is an indication here that ageing can lead to liberation from some types of discriminatory response; it is unlikely two younger women could share a similar kiss in a public space without a sense of risk. But how does this assumption translate to different types of situation? The de-sexing of later life can lead to gay and lesbian partnerships being cast as friendships, treated with less seriousness and not accorded the same status as heterosexual marriages. While ageist assumptions may prove benign in one context, they hold different implications elsewhere. This highlights a point to be taken up later in this chapter regarding the situated nature of discrimination and the meanings attached to encounters according to context.

The de-sexualisation of later life also has implications for heterosexual men. Narratives of age-related asexuality frame assumptions that older men are (literally) 'not up to it' and leave them open to judgement on this account. In this way, the fragility of heteronormative masculinity is highlighted based, as it is, on the unpredictable penis. With increasing attention focused upon maintaining an active sexual (intercourse) life and the availability of the chemical wherewithal to do so, the interviews suggested these men are also likely to judge themselves wanting on this basis. However, the contrasting narratives around male heterosexuality mean that different responses to changes in later life are possible. Some men may still gracefully (and perhaps with some relief or with some regret) accept what they see as their own de-sexualisation.

This twice-divorced man questioned the status of his current relationship due to an absence of intercourse:

Yeah, I've been in a relationship for two years ... but it isn't a sexual relationship as such because ... long-term diabetes has various effects, impotency being one of them. HM7(55)

When asked about his current sex life, he replied:

Pretty non-existent! This is primarily due the fact that an erection is now difficult to achieve ... These problems manifest themselves as a longer time to obtain an erection, and when it does arrive, a lack of firmness makes penetration difficult.... I find that my sexual desire has been replaced to a degree by many other things that I did not have or know about when I was younger. HM7(55)

There is a sense here of revision and rethinking of relationships in parallel with physical change. Other men sought to contest asexuality by demonstrating that they were still active in recognisably sexual ways:

When first married, we managed to enjoy intercourse at the rate of about twice a day for 300 days or so of the first year. Since then things have quietened down a little and we simply act as our fancy takes us. HM5(72)

Others redefine or challenge definitions of sexuality that depend solely on the continuation of penis-vagina sex within a loving or committed relationship. Sometimes there was hesitation over what counted as a sexual relationship:

I've been going with S... for about 10 years and we've never had a sexual relationship ... nevertheless we do know each other very well ... we have cuddled ... well, there is still a sexual thing there in terms of cuddling or just in terms of how you relate ... I mean the other person is a woman and you relate to her because she is different to you. Sexuality covers such a wide (range) ... it's not just sexual intercourse. I still feel as though I'm a sexual being in particular ways. HM3(68)

Dating

Most of the interviewees were single, many of them widowed or divorced. Both men and women commented on the difficulty of forming new relationships in later life. However, their reported experiences of seeking partners implied the dating 'market' offers an unequal experience for men and women, and one that foregrounds age in ways disadvantageous to women. Many interviewees signalled the discovery that age has a relative value attached when it comes to dating and is integral to the expedient way people are ranked or rated. Several of the heterosexual women noted that heterosexual men seemed to be looking for women who were significantly younger than themselves while younger heterosexual men didn't seem to be interested in older women. One described how she had used the Lonely Hearts column in a local newspaper:

If you read through the columns you will find a 70 year old man is always asking to meet a woman between 55 and 60. And I think that's probably because they're looking for somebody to look after them. ... all the men seem to want biddable females who will look after them or stop at home. HW1(73)

She did make contact with one man:

We were talking on the phone and we had got quite a lot in common and then he asked me how old I was and I told him and he went 'Oh', and I was four years older than him and then he said to me 'Well please tell me how would you treat a younger man?' and I said 'Well I'd just try not to wear him out' and I never heard from him again and it was solely because he thought I was four years older than him and that was an impossible situation. And that struck me as strange because he was a man on his own and we had so much in common, yet he didn't want to meet. HW1(73)

This experience suggests age can be interpreted almost as a tradable commodity and that men and women have unequal leverage in this context. Opportunities for forming new relationships are uneven, with older women having less choice and attributed less 'worth'. A number of gay men reported comparable experiences with the gay dating scene, with youth a valued asset contrasting to the derogation of older identities:

> *If you go on Gaydar* [a website for gay men] *and they give an age range 'I'm attracted to someone up to the age of 45'. Fine, I accept that but what I don't accept is when they write in their descriptions the kind of person they are looking for and say 'no oldies and wrinklies and people with pot bellies please'. That's a bloody insult.* GM1(59)

This observation reveals how open and apparently uncensored age discrimination can be on gay dating websites. In accessing such sites this respondent risks exposure to insulting and derisory references to ageing and older identities. When compared with the politics of heterosexual dating, this suggests that older gay men encounter discrimination premised upon negative judgements of appearance and the outward signs of ageing, in similar ways to older heterosexual women. For both, the sight or signs of 'oldness' devalue them in contexts where age has currency.

In regard to dating and accessing sexual spaces, the heterosexual men faced rather different issues. For most of them, marriage established a socially sanctioned 'space' within which sexuality could remain important.

> *The physical aspect remains important for me and ... very important for my wife. She's 81 ... We make love frequently, satisfactorily apart from the fact that I have no ejaculation ... I'm very active sexually.* HM1(87)

> *I married my second wife in 1999 and we have a brilliant life together. We both enjoy each other's bodies.* HM5(72)

Similarly, ongoing relationships were analogous to marriage in that they created a context in which there was no need to 'date'. Within such relationships the view was expressed that any attempts to find new partners would be disloyal. Marriage, or a long-term relationship, however, was not necessarily seen as precluding the need to explore other possibilities. This interviewee, while signalling fidelity in the context of his marriage, explored his sexuality through nudism and masturbation:

I'm a nudist so I tend not to wear clothes unless I absolutely have to and it's there ... Having an erect penis is a nice sensation. When I get home one of the first things I do is take my clothes off and the penis has a mind of its own, and a bit of masturbation certainly helps it get erect ... if I get bored I'm quite happy to sit there and play with myself and my wife's sitting there reading a book or whatever. HM4(58)

Similarly, Tom used Viagra and group sex to open up new sexual spaces:

I have had the good fortune recently of being involved in some small group sessions ... our bisexual neighbour remarked that the setting (his garden) was so secluded that we could have a three-way and nobody would notice. My partner admitted that she had never been in one and wondered what it would be like ... that led to more risqué banter that led to a ménage-a-trois for the rest of the afternoon and into the evening. Thanks to Viagra I was able to rise to the occasion. HM2(60)

Another of the (divorced) heterosexual men used role play to maintain a sex life. He responded to his inability to maintain an erection by devising alternative forms of sexual expression:

There are no signs of life in my penis at all. But I feel. I've got all the psychological feelings and all the desires, and I've got sensitivity in my penis. It just doesn't get hard. It doesn't get erect. HM3(68)

As a response to this situation, he reports:

I can't have penetrative sex, so just forget it. There's a little part of my character that enjoys two things ... first of all, I wear women's underwear ... I don't wear a bra but I wear women's briefs and when I'm in the house I wear a skirt ... so that's one thing and I get a lot of psychological satisfaction out of that, particularly if there's a lady comes to visit me ... at the same time I thought if I say to the ladies that I want to be caned or spanked ... then I might be able to persuade them to do it. HM3(68)

With these exceptions, however, the heterosexual male interviewees regarded a committed relationship as the only recognisable sexual space. It would be interesting to have had accounts of other sexual spaces available to and created by heterosexual men, not least because they might have shown whether their use indicates a compliance with the 'need' to remain active sexually, or whether they act as spaces for challenging the meaning of sexuality. Such accounts might also have revealed how permeable the boundaries are between heterosexuality and homosexuality. In this context, one heterosexual respondent said he had given talks about his views on nudism to a London gym whose clientele were mainly gay. Similarly other, nominally heterosexual men, described homosexual experiences at various points in their lives.

Image and appearance

The one thing I try very hard not to do is what I call dressing mutton up as lamb. I don't wear the garish make-up as I used to, slightly more gentle. HW6(67)

Intersections of age, sexuality and gender emerged in the interviews, both in the manner of reporting age discrimination and in the nature of the experiences described. Perhaps unsurprisingly, open-ended questions on sexuality and ageing elicited much talk of image, attractiveness and what were considered the challenges associated with ageing and self-presentation. One theme running across many of the interviews was how age is used as a point of reference in evaluating conduct and appearance. For instance a number of men talked of their concerns at being perceived and labelled 'dirty old man'. One heterosexual respondent reported chatting to a little girl in the local library he visits regularly and finding himself being questioned by the police as a result. Another felt that any form of sexual interest by an older man was seen as a perversion. In general however, unlike many of the women interviewees, few men attempted to see themselves through the eyes of others.

Many of the interviews with women included reference to how the outward and physical signs of ageing had a bearing upon social encounters. These signs of ageing were felt to be at odds with dominant notions of femininity, the implication being that contemporary constructions of the feminine rest upon the negation of age. Some of the women talked about the difficulty of finding clothes

57

they felt were appropriate for their age, that were attractive rather than frumpy. A number recalled the efforts of shop assistants to impose certain styles and described how such practices are strategically resisted:

> *When you go into a shop and say I'm looking for a blouse or a skirt or something, they do tend to bring out rather frumpy stuff if you're a bit older [...] instead of wearing comfortable clothes to go shopping in, you have to wear something dressed up to the nines just to say 'Well this is what I wear, what have you got in the same sort of thing?'* HW1(73)

This account suggests such encounters are a repeated and commonplace occurrence. It reveals a subtle and even mundane dimension to age discrimination. As shop assistants compel older women to consider the 'frumpy stuff', they implicitly uphold notions of what is acceptable for an older person and in so doing promote a uniform image.

Some older lesbians described an added layer to these everyday negotiations: the pressure to conform to certain notions of femininity in later life. They are forced to recognise that the image they seek is perceived by others to be transgressive.

> *I've got a very nice (hairdresser). I've been to him for ages but it took me ages to persuade him to cut my hair really short. It's not short now, I've changed my mind about that but he said, he kept saying to me 'You don't want to look too butch, do you?' and I said 'Yes, I don't mind looking butch.' You know, I just had to keep saying to him 'I do want to look butch actually' ... but clothes are very difficult because I do like clothes that are fairly masculine and in my, I'm short [laughs] and broad and [laughs] it's quite hard to find ... I often feel when I go into shops people are being, you know, 'what's she expecting to find here?'* L4(69)

In common with the study described in Chapter 3, such negotiations suggest that age is salient to these service encounters. The reproduction of images reveals something of the 'everyday' quality of intersecting forms of discrimination, illustrating ways in which shop workers and hairdressers operate as arbiters of both heteronormativity and age appropriateness regarding image and appearance. These unremarkable and routine encounters are shown to contain often direct forms of coercion: older women are pressured to adhere to certain ways of looking and presenting themselves. Notably, the images on offer are asexual or de-sexed, indeed the frumpiness referred to by several interviewees seems to advertise sexual disinterest.

Some women commented that finding attractive clothes in larger sizes is particularly difficult. Some thought this was a form of age discrimination but others indicated it was more a lack of awareness. Several also talked about skin care adverts and how they demonise ageing. One said that these adverts implied:

> ... that somehow ageing is a sin and you have to do everything you can not to show it. I do find that that is very, very discriminating. HW2(66)

Such comments underline how the social status of women is tied to appearance and they prompted discussion of ways of resisting this. For instance, some spoke of trying to appear happy and strong and thereby younger. Others felt grey hair has a de-sexualising effect, and conflicting opinions were registered over the strategy of hair-dyeing.

> But I sometimes say to younger women who are toying with that [dyeing their hair] and thinking what to do, that it does make a difference, it does make a difference if you are grey and they can think you are older than you are, or frumpier than you are. L6(63)

Tracking the association of hair with the politics of age, Gerike (1990) argues that the greater proportions of women who dye their hair, compared to men, is an indicator of the intersection of ageism with sexism. Her interpretation is that dyeing represents a form of 'passing', a way of associating with a group that enjoys greater privilege and prestige, perhaps not dissimilar to how some lesbians and gay men pass as heterosexual in order to avoid discrimination (Johnson 2002).

Many spoke of self-consciously performing new selves in order to resist being categorised as 'old'. Hair, clothes, make-up, and even behaviour and self-expression, were presented as resources in the tactical challenge to discriminatory encounters. Some interviewees felt altering their appearance could more accurately reflect what they felt and how they saw themselves. This is self-reconstruction aimed at challenging dominant perceptions. At the same time the interviews revealed that it is not possible to feel positive about dominant constructions of 'old-looking'. One woman, for example, drew our attention to an image designed to elicit humour.

> *There was a birthday card someone had given me, a friend of a friend. And she had her coat open, she had nothing on, she had breasts hanging about an inch above her knees and, erm, she had a horrible sort of look on her face, unhappy or whatever and this guy goes: 'Oh go on, show us your tits' ... and I thought, what? I felt really, you know I felt dirty and ashamed.* L1(69)

A number of women recalled occasions when friends or family had drawn attention to the physical signs of ageing, reinforcing wider messages about the unattractiveness of older bodies. Some expressed a dislike of their own ageing bodies. One woman, for example, spoke of how her negative feelings regarding her changing appearance influenced social and sexual encounters and her own sense of self:

> *I think people look at me as a big fat slob (laughs). To be quite honest, I do feel myself that I don't look attractive anymore, so what goes on in my head, other people are thinking the same thing as me, and that's probably why I don't get anywhere with anybody. Do you understand me? I can't get acquainted with anybody because the way I feel about myself is what I feel they are looking at, you know. ... I don't like my body anymore even though in my mind I would still like to have the sex side of it. My body, I hate my body now.* L5(65)

Self-evaluations like this reveal the effects and impact of discrimination but also something of its contradictions. While older women find themselves cast as de-sexed 'old ducks', there is a concomitant emphasis upon the grotesque in how older bodies are represented and perceived. Commonplace images such as those found on birthday cards are designed to prompt disgust at the sight of old age as part of the affective response associated with age discrimination. The sight of the older body and any suggestion of sexual activity in later life are thereby continually reiterated as repulsive or unthinkable. For example, in recalling a television programme one interviewee commented:

> *They were talking about being frightfully broadminded and talking about women sexually, and as far as they would get would be to aged 60, and after that they went dead silent … I mean it becomes distasteful for people to think about.* HW4(81)

(In)visibility

The 'dead silence' observed here also illustrates one of the more striking gendered contrasts in the data gathered for the study. Emphasis was placed by both lesbian and heterosexual women upon the issue of visibility - or more accurately, of being made to feel invisible. Indeed, invisibility is the challenge that Barbara Macdonald issues in the title of her book 'Look Me in the Eye' (Macdonald and Rich 1983): the often subtle process of social erasure that older women experience on a day to day basis. It was an experience echoed by many female interviewees:

> *The main problem of being older doesn't relate to being a lesbian, it's to do with obviously being older and being overlooked. I mean people simply look straight over your head or straight through you and they don't see you. So many older people have spoken of this, but when it happens to you, first of all you think, 'Goodness me, how interesting, how funny', and then sometimes I get cross and think what a cheek, you know, I could tell you a thing or two you can imagine. So for me that's the main problem, it's sort of not being taken into account, being invisible.* L6(63)

One or two women signalled that feeling invisible was not an entirely negative experience, they liked being able to observe others without being noticed. Others talked of realising how they were no longer the object of men's gaze. A sense of becoming invisible or 'looked through' applied not only to the domain of sexuality but also more broadly to social experiences of being an older woman.

Being made to feel invisible illustrates well the cumulative fashion in which many, often fleeting, encounters resonate to create a more forceful impression and sense of self. As the richly observant quote below outlines, 'invisibility' is interactionally achieved. It is something collectively 'done to' older people, often in ways that are subtle and oblique but nonetheless delivering a clear message about the value attached to old age.

> *Just a sense I get, whereas when I'm in an older group there's always a challenge there, a look in their eye* [laughs] *if you like. With younger people it's almost like, glance over and they've gone on to a younger woman, you know what I mean? You're not there, you're not as interesting as them, sexual stuff, but um then that's ok by me, but you still get that feeling, you know? … Looks maybe, in looks, you know sort of not even an eyebrow raised, it's almost like, look away immediately, and pick something up because they're embarrassed or they think it's not right. … You know it's almost like you're not there. And they just, they don't even look at you or talk to you, and if they do it's almost like 'what are you doing here?' You know.* L1(69)

The dynamic described by this interviewee gets to the heart of the concerns addressed in this chapter. The conduct described could hardly be considered extreme and yet the process by which this woman is made to feel she is 'not there' represents an absolute form of exclusion. In a study of everyday racism, Essed (1991) challenges dominant conceptions in her suggestion that the drama of racism is precisely this everyday quality and its reproduction via a host of often mundane practices. The issue of visibility implies parallels with how everyday forms of age discrimination might be interpreted.

IDENTITY, NETWORKS AND SUPPORT

Until recently, few models have existed to support an understanding of how care and support are negotiated within sexually dissident networks. Cronin (2006) argues that a long-standing but unacknowledged emphasis on heterosexual forms of social support in later life maintains the stereotype of the socially isolated and rejected older lesbian or gay man. More recently, notions such as 'friendship families' and 'chosen families' (Weston 1991) have become popular for describing how lesbians and gay men draw upon and invest in networks of friends and partners.

At times of biographical disruption, the uneven nature of support available to people is thrown into relief, with discrimination a shaping influence upon these conditions. One issue to emerge from the interviews was how certain life events increase a person's vulnerability to discrimination. A prominent example of this is bereavement. One gay man spoke of the absence of support from his neighbours while he cared for his dying partner, and the sense of uncertainty surrounding their willingness to assist.

I wonder sometimes just what my neighbours think and what my neighbours' attitude really is, and so if something went wrong how far they would be willing to offer support. My experience in terms of support on the basis of age and being gay is variable. Generally speaking when I was looking after, caring for, my partner we had virtually no support from our immediate neighbours, perhaps sympathetic but nothing more than that. GM3(64)

Following the death of his partner, he visited his local GP surgery and made an effort to seek support when at a low ebb:

I went to see my doctor who wasn't available that day so I saw another member of the practice and my notes were all there and I know that they're all there and, um, I was feeling really very low and physically not well either. And this doctor dealt with my physical issues and then I just sat there and I said to him 'Do you believe in dealing with people holistically?' which was a bit of a shock to him, to hear that, and he said 'Of course I do, is there anything else?' And I said 'Yes, I'm bereaved' and he said 'Oh, did you lose your wife?' and I was so angry at that stupid response that I just said 'No, it was my partner and I'm going, goodbye.' GM3(64)

Both formal and informal sources of help failed this man at a time when he was in need, illustrating the way discriminatory practices cut across multiple spheres of everyday living. One of the lesbian interviewees similarly described the social milieu of the rural area she lived in, where many people assumed her partner was 'just a friend'. When this partner subsequently died she recalls her sense of isolation.

I do think it's more difficult to get over when you're older, especially when you can't talk about it to anyone because they

63

*just don't want to know. The whispers have all gone round and
some will have thought 'Oh, that's rotten', and some will have
thought 'Oh well, it's just a friend, what's all the fuss about?'*
L8(74)

Accounts such as these offer insights into the particular implications
for sexual dissidents of the de-sexing of old age. It almost seems that
in the eyes of many others, including many service providers, older
lesbians and gay men do not exist (Pugh 2002). Denial of sexuality
implies a loss of identity, and such conditions are thrown into relief
at times of crisis or need.

The comparative design of this study served to inform an
understanding of the uneven implications of discrimination for the
different groupings of interviewees. The absence of support and in
some cases outright hostility of neighbours reported by gay and
lesbian interviewees, helps explain why many declined to invest in
traditional notions of community as tied to locale. Instead, access to a
broader sexual dissident community was obtained, often via
sexualised spaces, commonly in the form of commercial venues.
However, with age came an increasing sense of discomfort at the
unwelcoming atmosphere to older people in many of these settings:

I went to Trade (a night club) *with another older friend and,
um, a young guy came up to me, we were just sitting drinking,
and he said to me 'Can I kiss you, mister?' So I said, 'Why do
you want to do that?' So he said, 'Well I had a bet with my mate
over there, if I kiss you he'll buy me a pint.' That's insulting.*
GM2(72)

Funny enough the Glass Bar (a lesbian bar), *when I've been in
there, younger people come in but they go upstairs, so there's no
connection there because they are going to the dancing, you
know. Mainly, what it is, the older people are downstairs.*
L5(65)

Such accounts highlight the apparently open and unabashed nature
of age discrimination and segregation on the scene. Recounted
experiences included directly discriminatory responses from
gatekeepers such as bouncers and receptionists of various kinds, as
well as encounters with younger members of the clientele. How the
gay and lesbian press fail to address older people was also

highlighted, many noting that images of older people are entirely absent from their pages. Others commented on how clubs and bars advertise themselves in ways that are explicitly age-marked. Previous research into 'non-heterosexual' ageing reported similar experiences on the part of gay men:

> The pervasive story amongst older gay men is that visible signs of ageing can mark one as undesirable/unwelcome in gay culture.
>
> (Heaphy and Yip 2003:12)

As noted earlier, the temptation is to draw parallels between the experiences of age discrimination described by gay men and heterosexual women. However, findings from our study differ from this previous research to the extent that age discrimination was also reported as a feature of lesbian social networks and venues. This invites an interpretation that recognises the territorial nature of public spaces and how space is claimed, sometimes aggressively, by younger people. Indeed, it has been argued that, historically, the lesbian and gay scene has long served as a site of intergenerational conflict (Jennings 2006). Our lesbian and gay respondents certainly reported a sense of change to the places where they felt most comfortable:

> *I don't know when it happens and I am sure there are 60-plus women who go to the clubs and everything, but at some point, I think a lot of women think 'Do I really want to go down to central London and go where there are all these 18 year olds?' ... So you just find yourself drifting out of that circle of possibility into a much more day to day life I guess, and a social life which is with older friends or with project work.* L7(65)

Reflections such as this convey how the lesbian and gay scene is an age-marked territory. Many spoke of segregation between the generations both physically and socially, indicating the lateral nature of the networks to which they belonged (i.e. with people of similar ages). A number of people also noted the lack of age-inclusive spaces. While sexualised spaces serve as an alternative to heterosexualised public environments (Bell and Valentine 1995) and are often considered places of safety (Corteen 2002), the irony is that for older people they no longer represent an escape from discrimination and social rejection.

These, then, were the main topics discussed by interviewees as experiences of age discrimination in relation to sexuality. In the remainder of this chapter we turn to more methodological issues about how our side-by-side study design affected the sort of data that was generated.

GATHERING EVIDENCE ON DISCRIMINATION IN LATER LIFE: SOME CHALLENGES

Talk of sexuality

In designing our study we agreed that open-ended questions would help us understand how issues of sexuality and discrimination were perceived and made sense of by the people we interviewed. Inadvertently, this led to two fairly distinct if overlapping bodies of data. On the one hand the lesbian and gay interviewees referred to sexuality in terms of identity (often a fairly politicised one), shaped not least by a lifetime's experience of discrimination. The interviews generated discussion and reflection on what it is like to be an older gay man or lesbian as well as descriptions of and comparisons between the different forms of discrimination they faced.

> *It is what you do, the act or action, the activity and, say something like 'You are old so you are less of a human being', that kind of thing, in the same way that when you say 'You filthy queer', you know, 'You're queer. Queers should be strung up'... it is said with the same kind of violence.* GM1(59)

By contrast, the heterosexual interviewees talked of sexuality largely in individualised terms of feelings, desire, capacity and sexual practices, and rarely if ever made explicit reference to what it meant to be an older heterosexual or to heterosexuality as a coherent identity.

Talk of discrimination

When asked what the term 'age discrimination' suggested to them, many of the heterosexual men and women replied that it made them think of something analogous to 'race discrimination'. Initially, none of them identified sexuality as a sphere connected to the experience of age discrimination. However, when the topics on the interview schedule were explored, many did identify ways in which they felt that being older meant their sexuality was treated as non-existent, unimportant or ridiculous.

While few heterosexual participants used the language of 'age discrimination', most of them did talk about ways in which they felt they were discriminated against in relation to their sexuality because of their age. These were often quite subtle ways and there was some discussion of whether it should be described as age discrimination or as simple ignorance or lack of awareness. By contrast, for many of the lesbian and gay interviewees, discriminatory encounters were easily recalled and cited, often in detail.

Perhaps the subtlety of discrimination exercised against older heterosexual men is in part evidence of their privileged status. However, an increased focus on male sexual performance may lead to change. It also has implications for the recognition of discrimination. If older men are placed under increasing expectations to perform and to use the technology that is supposed to ensure performance, then it could be that many will develop a clearer perception of age discrimination in relation to their sexuality than at present.

The interviews conducted with gay men and lesbians generated many accounts of age discrimination that were striking not only for their detail but also the way they explained more subtle and embedded practices. By examining black women's accounts of racism, Essed (1991) concludes that repeated experiences of discrimination over time lead to a sophisticated awareness of and ability to recognise and articulate all forms of discriminatory experience. Contrasts between the reported experiences of gay and lesbian interviewees and those of the heterosexual participants, suggest this interpretation may apply here. Longstanding experience of discrimination perhaps means older lesbians and gay men are more attuned to and better able to label such encounters in later life.

However, an alternative explanation would be that these differences are an artefact. The decision to match interviewers as far as possible with interviewees in terms of sexual orientation undoubtedly facilitated access to interviewees in the first place, especially for the lesbian and gay participants. But different interviewers naturally have different styles and approaches, especially when undertaking semi-structured interviews. These differences might be sufficient to account for the differences between our data sets. We hope to explore this issue further in future work.

DISCUSSION

A prerequisite for all forms of prejudice is the assumption that members of a particular group are essentially the same. The impression that older people, through ageing, grow to share certain attributes, patterns of behaviour, appearance and beliefs, is a cornerstone of ageism. Often, it is the powerful signifying quality of the appearance of old age that triggers a discriminatory response: according to Ahmed (2004: 55), 'the *perception* of a group in the body of the individual'. One interviewee commented:

> *Over the years, increasingly to this point I thought 'Do you know, is there some sort of prejudice or am I getting paranoid?' Because if you think people aren't liking you, you obviously think 'They don't like me', so it's a sort of paranoia. And then you think 'Well, I was never like that before and I always got on very well with nearly everybody' ... Anyway the thing is, I realised there really was. One or two of my friends would say 'Well, don't you realise it's because we're, you know, old ducks in the eyes of the rest of the world', sort of thing.* L8(74)

This particular quote illustrates well some of our concern with what constitutes 'everyday discrimination'. The dawning realisation, albeit an uncertain one, of 'some sort of prejudice' suggests not a discrete event but a host of experiences that resonate with one another to create an impression. The interviewee talks of how the tenor of social encounters has altered as she has aged, suggesting that the process of ageing is embedded within relationships. Becoming an 'old duck' is something achieved via the repetition of social encounters, difficult for this interviewee to pinpoint or isolate but a sense, shared by her friends, of their growing uniformity in the eyes of others. The quote also underlines the way this process upturns a sense of self and leads to questions about worth and how we are regarded. Terms like 'old duck' convey a strong sense of the discrimination that lies behind much of the accounts considered in this chapter. Not simply are older people under pressure to conform to inflexible generalisations but these are derogatory, demeaning identities to occupy. Notably, 'old ducks' are devoid of any sexual connotations, they are inherently asexual, unthreatening and benign.

Even where alternative sexual identities appear to be on offer, these still have the effect of creating subject positions for older people. Thus, pharmacological interventions like Viagra may appear to offer men (heterosexual and gay) the opportunity to recreate youthful virility. It may be true that such products have ushered in a greater willingness to discuss male sexuality (Marshall 2006; Potts 2004). But it is also the case that such discussion has led to the colonisation of ageing male sexuality as a newly medicalised realm controlled by doctors and large pharmaceutical companies (Marshall and Katz 2002).

This study has illustrated the significance of how meaning is attached to particular encounters. At times, discrimination can be subtle, even delicately handled during social interaction. Descriptions such as 'not even an eyebrow raised, it's almost like, look away immediately, and pick something up because they're embarrassed or they think it's not right' (L1) reveal the importance of understanding the 'situated production of prejudice' (Speer and Potter 2000). Rather than assuming that discrimination lies in the use of certain terms or particular practices, it is the way meaning is attached in the context of social encounters that creates the effect of discrimination.

The variable nature of the impact of discrimination was revealed in these interviews. Talk of life events such as bereavement or the onset of illness suggests that these can act as catalysts. For some interviewees, moments of crisis uncovered discrimination, for instance through revealing an absence of support when needed. They were times when discrimination could have the most damaging impact. Others however, most notably the heterosexual men, found it difficult to identify instances of discrimination. This can be seen as a consequence of the relatively privileged position that they have occupied, but this should not obscure the changing dynamics of what 'counts' as male sexuality. In particular, the expectation (if not compulsion) that they demonstrate on-going and narrowly defined sexual activity is changing the definition of male sexuality, and this is likely to have implication for all sexualities.

These accounts draw attention to how changing forms of discrimination, social rejection and exclusion function in the context of biographical narratives. They underline the way events in different areas of life interact and lead to responses that range from an unthinking acceptance of powerful narratives to personal explorations that begin to challenge previous assumptions.

REFERENCES

Ahmed, S. (2004) *The Cultural Politics of Emotion*, New York: Routledge.

Arber, S., Davidson, K. and Ginn, J. (eds) (2003) *Gender and Ageing: Changing Roles and Relationships*, Maidenhead: Open University Press.

Arber, S. and Ginn, J. (eds) (1995) *Connecting Gender and Ageing: A Sociological Spproach*, Buckingham: Open University Press.

Bell, D. and Valentine, G. (1995) Introduction: orientation, in Bell, D. and Valentine, G. (eds) *Mapping Desire: Geographies of Sexualities*, London: Routledge.

Calasanti, T. and Slevin, J.F. (2001) *Gender, Social Inequalities, and Aging*, Oxford: AltaMira Press.

Copper, B. (1988) *Over the Hill: Reflections on Ageism Between Women*, California: Crossing Press.

Corteen, K. (2002) Lesbian safety talk: problematizing definitions and experiences of violence, sexuality and space, *Sexualities*, 5(3), 259–80.

Cronin, A. (2006) Sexuality in Gerontology: a heteronormative presence, a queer absence, in Daatland, S.O. and Biggs, S. (eds) *Ageing and Diversity: Multiple Pathways and Critical Migrations*, Bristol: Policy Press.

Essed, P. (1991) *Understanding Everyday Racism: An Interdisciplinary Theory*, London: Sage.

Gerike, A.E. (1990) On gray hair and oppressed brains, in Rosenthal, E.R. (ed.) *Women, Aging and Ageism*, New York: Harrington Park Press.

Gott, M. (2005) *Sexuality, Sexual Health and Ageing*, Maidenhead: Open University Press.

Gullette, M.M. (1997) *Declining to Decline: Cultural Combat and the Politics of the Midlife*, Charlottesville, VA: University Press of Virginia.

Hajek, C. and Giles, H. (2002) The old man out: an intergroup analysis of intergenerational communication among gay men, *Journal of Communication*, December.

Heaphy, B. and Yip, A. (2003) Uneven possibilities: understanding non-heterosexual ageing and the implications of social change, *Sociological Research Online*, 8(4).

Heaphy, B., Yip, A. and Thompson, D. (2003) *Lesbian, Gay Bisexual Lives Over 50*. ESRC funded project report, Nottingham: York House Publications.

Heaphy, B., Yip, A. and Thompson, D. (2004) Ageing in a non-heterosexual context, *Ageing and Society*, 24, 881–902.

Jennings, R. (2006) The Gateways Club and the emergence of a post-second world war lesbian subculture, *Social History*, 31(2), 206–25.

Johnson, C. (2002) Heteronormative citizenship and the politics of passing, *Sexualities*, 5(3), 317–36.

Jones, J. and Pugh, S. (2005) Ageing gay men: lessons from the sociology of embodiment, *Men and Masculinities*, 7(3), 248–60.

Jones, R.L. (2002) 'That's very rude, I shouldn't be telling you that': older women talking about sex, *Narrative Inquiry,* 12(1), 121–42.

Jones, R.L. (2006) 'Older people' talking as if they are not older people: Positioning Theory as an explanation, *Journal of Ageing Studies*, 20(1), 79–91

Katz, S. and Marshall, B. (2003) New sex for old: lifestyle, consumerism and the ethics of aging well, *Journal of Aging Studies*, 17, 3–16.

Macdonald, B. and Rich, C. (1983) *Look Me in the Eye: Old Women, Aging and Ageism*, Denver, CO: Spinster Ink Books.

Marshall, B. and Katz, S. (2002) Forever functional: sexual fitness and the ageing male body, *Body and Society*, 8(4), 43–70.

Marshall, B. (2006) The new virility: Viagra, male aging and sexual function, *Sexualities*, 9(3), 345–62.

Potts, A. (2000) The essence of the hard on: hegemonic masculinity and the cultural construction of 'erectile dysfunction', *Men and Masculinities*, 3(1), 85–103.

Potts, A. (2004) Deleuze on Viagra (or what can a 'Viagra-body' do?) *Body and Society*, 10(1), 17–36.

Pugh, S. (2002) The forgotten: a community without a generation – older lesbians and gay men, in Richardson, D. and Seidman, S. (eds) *Handbook of Lesbian and Gay studies*, London: Sage.

Schaffer, R.S. (1972) Will you still need me when I'm 64? in Jay, A. and Young, A. (eds) *Out of the Closets: Voices of Gay Liberation*, London: GMP Publisher.

Sontag, S. (1979) The double standard of aging, in Williams, J.H. (ed.) *Psychology of Women: Selected Readings*, New York: Norton.

Speer, S. and Potter, J. (2000) The management of heterosexist talk: conversational resources and prejudiced claims, *Discourse and Society*, 11(4), 543–72.

Wahler, J. and Gabbay, S.G. (1997) Gay men ageing: a review of the literature, *Journal of Gay and Lesbian Social Services*, 6(3), 1–20.

Ward, R., Vass, A.A., Aggarwal, N., Cybyk, B. and Garfield, C. (2005) A Kiss is Still a Kiss? – The construction of sexuality in dementia care, *Dementia*, 4(1), 49–72.

Weston, K. (1991) *Families We Choose: Lesbians, Gays, Kinship*, New York: Columbia University Press.

Woodward, K. (1999) *Figuring Age: Women, Bodies, Generations*, Bloomington: Indiana University Press.

5

CONSTRUCTIONS OF AGE/AGEISM AND DISABILITY/DISABLISM
Mapping some similarities and differences

CHIH HOONG SIN

INTRODUCTION

When it came to writing the paper on which this chapter is based, I found myself moving significantly away from its original title of 'Disability and impairment in later life'. Instead, emphasis fell squarely on the intersections between ageism and (dis)ablism. This reflects a fundamental belief in the need to look beyond individuals and their inherent and/or ascribed characteristics to examine the wider societal structures in which they are embedded in order to understand discriminations.

At the moment in time when Britain is moving towards the birth of the Commission for Equality and Human Rights (CEHR), it is of vital importance to look at how the various equality strands converge as well as diverge. Charged with promoting equality and combating discrimination(s), the CEHR has its work cut out in terms of making sense of the enormously complex motivations and manifestations of a range of discriminatory behaviour. This paper takes as its premise an exploration of how constructions of 'disability'/'disabled people' and 'old age'/'older people' (and correspondingly of (dis)ablism and ageism) can demonstrate similarities as well as differences. It behoves us to look more closely at what may be commonalities across different types of discriminations, and also to acknowledge what may be unique to particular equality strands. This will hopefully help inform coherent strategies to combat discrimination(s).

WHAT IS DISABILITY AND WHO IS A DISABLED PERSON?

It is quite common, in my professional role, to be asked the question: 'who are disabled people?' or 'what is a disability?'. Disability is a component of identity that is amorphous and potentially fluid. Yet, disability is still associated with the image of 'white sticks' and wheelchairs. Worryingly, the annual 'Attitudes and Awareness' surveys of the Disability Rights Commission (DRC) which was discontinued after the 2003 survey, demonstrated progressively lower proportions of respondents indicating awareness of the Disability Discrimination Act (DDA) as well as what the Act covers (DRC 2001, 2002, 2003a). Many remain unable to grasp fully what disability means and how it may be defined. The DRC Attitudes and Awareness surveys, for instance, point to extremely variable understandings of what disability covers apart from obvious physical conditions.

There are many definitions of disability and different ways in which it is conceptualised and operationalised in terms of data collection. Unlike developments in 'race'/ethnicity, there is as yet no harmonised question for the collection of information relating to disability (DRC 2005a). Many national household surveys do not provide adequate samples (and hence reliable estimates) of the disabled population and often only include individuals living in private households, thereby systematically excluding a range of disabled people who may be residing in other residential settings.

Perhaps more frustrating is the fact that existing questions that are perceived to cover 'disability' often conflate it with ill health and infirmity. In addition to problematic question wordings, the conflation of disability and health is more apparently demonstrated in the observation that 'disability question(s)' are often found within the 'health' section of survey instruments.

The paucity of good quality and consistent data on disability has meant that research has had to utilise a range of datasets that are not always compatible in terms of sample composition and/or how disability has been operationalised in data collection. The DRC itself currently draws on a range of national household surveys for disability data. Its widely disseminated 'Disability Briefing', draws largely on data originating from the Labour Force Survey (LFS) while referencing, in parts, data from the Family Resources Survey (FRS) (see DRC 2005b). Different source data are also called upon to support statements on particular sub-groups. For example, the DRC uses the FRS for estimates on disabled children, as the LFS (while used in the Disability Briefing) does not collect any information on children since its focus is very much on adults within the statutory working age. It is easy, therefore, to see the potential for confusion in relation to estimates of the disabled population.

There can often be a lack of appreciation that different estimates can arise from different ways in which disability is defined in various surveys. According to the DDA, disability is defined as 'a physical or mental impairment which has a substantial and long-term adverse effect on [a person's] ability to carry out normal day-to-day activities'. While this may appear initially to be rather straightforward, there are very real uncertainties around the many core components of this definition; for instance relating to what constitutes 'impairment', 'substantial', 'long-term', 'adverse', 'normal', and 'day-to-day activities'.

Very few existing surveys include questions covering the DDA definition of disability. Even when a DDA-compliant definition is allegedly used, the wording can vary significantly. There can thus be different resultant estimates of the number of disabled people (Twomey *et al.* 2005). For instance, the Department for Work and Pensions (DWP) introduced a question on disability in the 2002/03 Family Resources Survey that they claimed was based on the DDA definition. The question read:

> Do you have any long-standing physical or mental illness, health problem or disability? By long-standing I mean anything that has troubled you over a period of time or that is likely to affect you over a period of time?

Those who answer 'yes' are then asked if the declared illness or disability limits their activities in any way and in what areas of life.

The LFS, another purportedly DDA-compliant survey, uses a series of questions that read as follows:

> Do you have any health problems or disabilities that you expect will last more than a year?

If respondents answer 'yes', they are then asked what kind of health problem or disability they have based on a list. They are further asked if the declared health problems or disability, taken singly or together, substantially limit their ability to carry out normal day to day activities.

WHO IS AN 'OLDER PERSON'?

As in the case of disability and disabled people, there is recognition that the term 'older people' does not refer to a homogeneous group. Tinker (1997) argues that the definition of the term 'elderly' is centred on retirement (itself an arbitrary threshold of economic productivity). Walker (1980) and Phillipson (1982) are amongst those who have critiqued this social construction of structured dependency, an issue to be explored later in the chapter.

Instead, discussion turns here to the literature pertaining to minority ethnic older people in order to exemplify the fluidity of constructions of old age. Several writers have pointed out that chronological age is a poor indication of ageing in many minority ethnic communities. It is generally accepted in the literature that the 'ageing process' may start sooner within minority ethnic groups due to a combination of various factors including poorer health, lower socio-economic status, and poorer living environments. For such groups, 55 or even 50 has been taken as a more appropriate (albeit still arbitrary) age threshold, beyond which someone can be considered 'old'. This has been closely aligned with the theory of 'double jeopardy', first advanced by Dowd and Bengston (1978: 427) who argued that older people from minority ethnic backgrounds suffer a double burden of the 'devaluation of old age' and the 'additional economic, social and psychological burdens of living in a society in which racial equality remains ... a myth'.

The cultural context of age and ageing cannot be ignored. The journalist and writer Yasmin Alibhai-Brown candidly discussed how her mother 'chose' to be an old person at the age of 36:

> To be a woman in my community and young was often so arduous that many women yearned to reach the status of their mothers and mothers-in-law. So they developed aches, pains and deliberately slowed movements; spoke frequently about their failing bodies and the importance of herbal potions to keep them going.
>
> (Alibhai-Brown 1998: 24)

This candid observation of age and ageing indicates that growing old can be intimately associated with landmarks in one's life to do with changing roles and status: for instance, in becoming a grandmother.

Such individual perception of age and ageing is conditioned by the wider cultural context. For instance, Foong *et al.* (2000) described how turning 50 is perceived as having crossed the threshold and become 'elderly' by Chinese communities.

CONSTRUCTIONS OF IDENTITIES

The above are extremely brief accounts of the hugely complex fields of defining 'disabled' and 'old'. Nonetheless, the two preceding sections allude to some common ground between the two. It is important to note that these definitions are necessarily social constructions that give meaning and imbue characteristics to groups of people. As such they are at once structured and structuring. The accounts above suggest that both disability and age (as well as disablism and ageism) are often viewed and constructed through lenses tinted with a range of economic considerations as well as through lenses of disadvantage and need. While manifested in different ways, these often coalesce (in both cases) into constructions of disabled and/or older persons through negative caricatures characterised by their being allegedly net beneficiaries of a range of financial and non-financial support. Such caricaturing often positions these groups as targets of allegedly 'benign paternalism' a response with the potential to be both patronising and disempowering.

Unlike racism, however, the prejudice surrounding disabled people and older people arguably stem from somewhat different motivations. As Fennell *et al.* (1988) noted for social gerontology, many are 'well-disposed' towards older people causing them to want to know about 'their problems'. However, this 'benign interest' can manifest itself as a tendency to 'welfarise' the group under study. Welfarising often involves a mix of diminution and patronage. More importantly, it focuses on 'actions to meet need rather than ... attempt to discover the social processes which produce need' (Fennell *et al.* 1988: 6). This observation also holds true for perspectives on disabled people.

One of the results of such welfarising tendencies is that individuals labelled as 'disabled' and/or 'old' can often be defined primarily (or even solely) in terms of those labels. A parallel, and often more subtle, process simultaneously attaches a series of other characteristics onto the primary social identifier. Reductionism operates in both cases where groups of people (i.e. 'old' or 'disabled') are first constructed as being internally homogeneous. They are then assigned similar in-group characteristics. This allows them to be comfortably (re)presented as 'others' (see Goldberg 1993 for a similar argument in relation to cultural racism). In this way, both 'older people' and 'disabled people' can often be portrayed as not being quite the 'whole persons' that members of the 'general population' somehow are. This can be detected, for instance, in the practice of comparing various sets of statistics pertaining to either group against those of the 'general population' where the latter is implicitly held as the unproblematised 'norm'. Any difference is then often posited as a 'deviation from the norm': a 'deviance'.

Another manifestation of how this process operates can be found in the reactions towards the inclusion/exclusion of segments within those populations. The following extract from Fennell *et al.* (1988: 7) makes the case in relation to older people:

> Elderly people who do not fit into the pathology model (the rich, fit, active elderly person, the assertive elderly person, the political leader, the quiet, healthy busy elderly person, anyone getting on with a purposive existence) are almost defined out of frame. They are not a problem, they have no obvious needs, hence they cannot really be elderly.

Similarly, the majority of people covered by the DDA in Britain can be viewed as largely 'invisible' in the sense that the general public is sceptical of someone claiming to be 'disabled' if there are no obvious outward, and often physical, signs of disability (Grewal *et al.* 2002). It is of interest to note that this process also operates in the 'race' field. I have noted elsewhere (Sin 2004a, 2004b) the tendency to equate, usually implicitly, ethnic minorities with disadvantage. For instance, the fourth Policy Studies Institute survey of ethnic minorities in Britain bears the telling subtitle: *Diversity and Disadvantage* (Modood *et al.* 1997). A review of sampling approaches employed in studies of older people from minority ethnic groups in Britain has also revealed the common, but largely unexamined, deprivation and disadvantage biases underlying a variety of such approaches (Sin 2004b). Studies on minority ethnic groups thus 'tend to view the subjects as being different (and thus worthy of exclusive attention) or problematic (most often deprived or disadvantaged)'

(Sin 2004b: 267). Raj (2003), in this context, lamented the lack of studies on middle-class Asians in Britain. Middle-class ethnic minorities tend to be hollowed of the usual ethnicity-culture-identity equation applied uncritically to their counterparts in lower socio-economic positions. They have thus fallen out of the purview of British 'ethnic' studies.

A natural alliance?

It is a truism to note that Britain has an ageing population. It is also a truism to state that the incidence of disability and ill health increases with age, with the association rising steeply amongst those aged 80 and over. A report by the Social Exclusion Unit (2004) noted, for instance, that those aged 75 and over were the most likely to experience ill health or disability, and were among the most likely to experience multiple disabilities. Some types of impairment increase markedly with age, including hearing and sight problems as well as mobility difficulties (DWP 2005). The RNID, for instance, released figures showing that the incidence of deafness increases sharply from around the age of 50: 55 per cent of those aged 60 and over are reportedly deaf or hard of hearing (DoH 2004; RNID 2005). Mental health problems, in particular, have been shown to be more prevalent amongst older age groups, particularly those from lower socio-economic background (ONS 2004).

Data from the General Household Survey (GHS) also indicate that the proportion of older people reporting a long-standing health condition has increased. Between 2001 and 2002, the proportion of those aged 75 and over with a long-standing health condition increased from 63 to 72 per cent (ONS 2004). Even this, as some have argued, may be a gross under-estimation of true prevalence as the GHS only samples private households and leaves out those living in communal establishments. This latter group tends to display the highest rates of prevalence of chronic conditions.

Given the demographic and physiological contexts, why have the movements combating ageism and disablism not demonstrated greater affinity with each other and developed meaningful and sustained partnership working? For instance, the disability rights movement has traditionally regarded itself as distinct from campaigns around older people's rights. The DRC itself has recently expressed uncertainty as to whether the older population with impairments will necessarily associate with the disability rights movement. In the document *Shaping the Future of Equality*, the DRC (2005c) posed the question 'will they be competitors or allies for limited public resources?'

This question is not rhetorical. The assumed association between age and disability based on demographic trends and projections may not be as unproblematic as on first inspection. In relation to age and disability, it has been found that surveys on age often under-estimate the incidence of disability as older people have a tendency not to regard themselves as 'disabled' even when various impairments are reported. These are widely regarded as being a natural consequence of ageing. Priestley (2002) has demonstrated that disability is experienced differently across the life course. Even within more radical debates on disability rights, older people are rarely considered 'disabled' in quite the same way as younger adults and children. The stigma associated with disability is yet another disincentive for self-identification (Traynor and Walker 2003). Grewal *et al.* (2002), for instance, showed that less than half of respondents who would have, objectively, met the DDA definition of disability, did not declare themselves disabled.

A curious situation has arisen where, instead of the potential for multiple identifications, the categories of 'old' and 'disabled' have become somewhat mutually exclusive. Townsend (1981) and Priestley (2000), amongst others, have noted that since disability is often seen as a fact of life for many older people, they do not need to be 'othered' from their status as older people if they become disabled. In other words, it is enough to have been 'othered' once. As the movements combating discrimination in relation to ageism and disablism have progressed, older people can often find themselves in the position of having to choose between positive disability identities within the disability rights movement and potentially losing contact with other networks and other ways of defining their identities (Priestley 2002). It is telling that the DRC's Attitudes and Awareness surveys consistently demonstrated that people aged 65 and over have the lowest levels of awareness of the DDA: only 32 per cent in 2002.

This disassociation of old age and disability is also reflected in, and has been buttressed by, policy imperatives that have focused largely on disabled individuals of statutory working age, even though a significant proportion of disabled people are in fact over this age (Zarb and Oliver 1993).

DISABLISM AND AGEISM: SOME SIMILARITIES AND DIFFERENCES

It is important to note, however, that while there are overlaps in the forces driving disablism and ageism, there are also significant differences. In addition, manifest discriminatory behaviour that may appear similar could be motivated by quite different underlying forces. Some of these are discussed in the remainder of this paper using two examples that have resonance in studies relating to ageing and to disability.

Living independently

The concept of independent living has a longer history of development in relation to older people but has certainly taken on fresh momentum in the field of disability rights (see DRC 2006). In the field of social gerontology, there is a well-established concern with defining and understanding older people's informal support, often couched in terms of the concept of 'community care' although, as Johnson (1999) and others have noted, its meaning shifted from one of care *in* the community to one denoting care *by* the community.

Consequently, both Conservative and Labour governments have espoused the ideal of 'rolling back' the state as a direct provider of support and care services to older people. Informal community networks were seen as 'more responsive to real human need than the bureaucratic structures of the modern welfare state' (d'Abbs 1982: 8). Through a series of policy shifts, the provision of formal services for older people has been increasingly commodified and offered within the structures of a private market. The New Labour government elected in 1997 has moved it towards a mixed economy of care where services are provided by the state, the private sector, the voluntary sector and the informal sphere through complex combinations. The shifts in the provision of formal sources of support for older people have been covered comprehensively by many (e.g. Easterbrook 2003; Johnson 1999; Laing and Buisson 2001; Sin 2006).

Local authorities have moved from being direct providers to being purchasers of services. Their role has become one of needs assessment followed by putting in place arrangements that ensured such needs were met. Their performance against set standards and targets are regularly reviewed and monitored. Social services departments, similarly, were tasked to be 'the designers, organizers and purchasers of non-health care services, and not primarily as direct providers, making the maximum possible use of voluntary and private sector bodies' (Griffiths 1988: 1).

Johnson (1999) suggested that these various changes can be understood in the context of the communitarian ideology promoted by the New Labour government since 1997. This espoused self-reliance and the empowerment of individuals (with support) to take responsibility for their own welfare. The family was also seen as the central social aggregate for the provision of support and care (Driver and Martell 1997). In addition, mutual aid and self-help were encouraged. The role of the state then becomes one of facilitator, enabler and regulator.

The concept of living independently is far wider than the question of whether someone lives in an institutional setting or at home. An individual who is living at home may not be living independently. For instance, transport is a key element of social inclusion, with mobility being a vital component of the ability to live independently. Unfortunately, for both older people and disabled people, transport is often not available or accessible for their needs. The Disabled Persons' Transport Advisory Committee (2002) noted that inaccessible transport has a disproportionate adverse impact on disabled people, resulting in the fact that disabled people travel a third less than non-disabled people. Similarly, older people can be isolated due to inaccessible transport. A significant proportion of older people have a physical disability or long-standing health problem that makes it difficult for them to use a range of public transport. This can have an effect on their participation in a range of activities (DRC 2003b).

Likewise it must not be assumed that, just because a person is living in an institution, independent living becomes irrelevant. A recent study of older people in Britain (Gabriel and Bowling 2004) found that over two-thirds of their respondents emphasised the importance of retaining independence and saw this as an important factor in influencing their quality of life. This is true even for frail older people living in institutional care (Tester *et al.* 2004). An individual's perception of independence is dynamic and can change with age and/or circumstances (e.g. onset of disability). This has been documented for disabled pensioners (Godfrey *et al.* 2004). Independence can be understood as maintaining a sense of autonomy even when a person's ability to do things on his/her own may be compromised.

A more needs-led approach, involving some degree of user involvement, is becoming apparent in service provision for older people, particularly in terms of supporting them to live independently. The same cannot be said however for disabled (older) people where the numbers of people with learning disabilities or mental health needs in residential care has increased. While disabled people can, in theory, direct their personal assistance support in a way that suits their chosen lifestyles, this is often thwarted in the practice of community care assessment. Existing policies and services place undue emphasis on assessments of a person's 'vulnerability' (with a functional view of independence) and the potential risks which they may pose either to themselves or to others (Campbell 2004). Disabled people are therefore cast as 'vulnerable' and needing protection and care.

Some disabled people are therefore moved into residential care against their will, largely due to inflexible service provision. This situation is one of several discriminatory scenarios highlighted in a recent DRC advertising campaign 'Are We Taking The Dis?' The caption on one of its ads read: 'I'm disabled, so they've put me in a home' (DRC 2006). This highlights the often inappropriate 'solutions' put in place to address the perceived needs of disabled people. For example, the housing support charity, John Grooms, reported in 2003 that around 8,000 young adults were living in care homes primarily designed for older people. There seems to be dramatic increases in the numbers of those with learning difficulties and mental health problems being accommodated within local authority supported residential and nursing care (cited in Campbell 2004). The DRC has also handled legal cases involving involuntary institutionalisation (BBC, 4 March 2004).

Employment

Both disabled people and older people are often thought of as net beneficiaries rather than contributors. The definition of old age in relation to retirement is, however, becoming increasingly untenable. With the pensioner population rising in Britain, coupled with an ageing demographic profile, the concept of work is widely seen as needing to be more flexible. There have been controversies about further raising the age of retirement (Robinson and Banks 2005). Godfrey *et al.* (2004) have reported frustration among older people over there being limited employment opportunities available to them. The Government has responded by introducing age discrimination legislation in 2006.

In regard to disabled people, data from the LFS show that around half of the disabled people of working age were unemployed, many of whom wanted to work (DRC 2005b). This figure can be broken down by impairment. People with mental health problems have the lowest employment rates of all at just 21 per cent. One of the main reasons seems to be the resistance of employers to employing people with certain mental health conditions.

It is important to note that the majority of disabled people experience the onset of disability sometime during adulthood. Bardasi *et al.* (2000) estimated that around three per cent of those in work each year become 'limited in daily activities'. Evidence shows that one in six of those who become disabled while in work, lose their jobs during the first year after becoming disabled. Once out of work and on benefits, the structure of the welfare system around disability can often be a disincentive or prevent individuals from seeking employment. For instance, to be entitled to receipt of Incapacity Benefit (IB), individuals have to prove that they are incapable of work every day that they are in receipt of the benefit. Compulsory work-focused interviews, a means of getting IB claimants to get back into employment, however involves an odd combination of asking claimants to demonstrate their incapacity to work while simultaneously discussing their capacity to work. In the context of uncertainty, many claimants of IB are fearful of losing their entitlements. In addition, individuals falling within certain impairment types are regarded as 'more incapacitated' than others and hence exempt from initiatives of getting people back into employment.

Discrimination based on age and/or disability within employment is often motivated by a perceived lack of particular qualities or abilities (i.e. the lack is defined as a negative). For instance, ageism in employment practices can be couched in terms of redundancy of skills due to age, the reduction in capacity (particular mental capacity) to work, the loss of learning ability and being increasingly prone to making mistakes or being forgetful (Harper and Thane 1989: 52–3). Likewise the word 'disabled' itself, conveys the meaning that someone is 'less able' in various ways. Research with small employers commissioned by the DRC (2004) found that one quarter of those surveyed indicated that they thought employing a disabled person would incur additional costs, while over one-third think that disabled people would take more sick leave. Forty-five per cent of those surveyed also reported that it would be 'quite' or 'very difficult' to employ a disabled person. This figure was considerably higher than for the employment of older people. For older disabled people, the situation is worse. The Strategy Unit (2005) estimated that a quarter of disabled people experience (additional) discrimination in the labour market due to age.

Nonetheless, while discrimination on the grounds of age and disability within employment are often based on perceived negative qualities associated with age and disability, affecting the employability of individuals in these groups, the discrimination against disabled people often displays an additional concern: that disabled employees can pose a hazard to other employees. This is manifested, in some cases, in health and safety considerations whereby the employment of disabled people is perceived to be an unacceptable risk to the health and safety of other members of staff. People with mental health problems are often susceptible to such negative assessments. The DRC (2003c) amongst others have demonstrated that the coverage of mental ill health in the popular press and media tends to be very negative and inaccurate. They have often been portrayed as a menace to society or public order. Derogatory words such as 'nutter' and 'loony' can sometimes be used in the tabloids to describe people with mental health conditions (Ward 1997), with a further suggestion of association with violence.

Less apparent are the effects of a range of 'fitness to practice' guidelines that can be rather vague in the definition of 'fitness'. This leaves the guidelines open to interpretation. Therefore, a range of implicit and often individually-made decisions can have wide-ranging influence on the ability of disabled people to register, train and qualify in a range of professions.

While both older people and disabled people may be portrayed as net beneficiaries rather than contributors, particularly in the narrowly defined economic sense, the movement against age discrimination has had considerable success in repositioning older people as economic assets and providers. Data from the GHS for example have been used effectively to demonstrate the persistent finding that older people provide very significant amounts of care to other household members (e.g. Arber and Ginn 1991; Cooper *et al.* 1999). It is also a widely documented fact that older people contribute immensely in terms of volunteering activities. Both these forms of contribution have tangible economic benefits to wider society and have been variously quantified. In addition, the role of older people as direct providers of financial support cannot be overlooked not least given that younger people are widely reported to be looking to their parents for assistance in getting a foothold on the housing ladder.

In comparison, the disability rights movement has not performed as well in repositioning the debate around disabled people as net contributors as opposed to beneficiaries. The discussion, very much, still focuses on the cost of supporting disabled people in terms of benefits and service provision.

CONCLUSION

This paper has attempted to cover a highly complex terrain by looking at the construction of identities around being 'old' and 'disabled'. In particular, it has demonstrated how the portrayal and definition of both groups in terms of dependency and lack can lead to a range of discrimination. The ways in which ageism and disablism are manifested in everyday life have been explored, paying attention to similarities and differences in patterns and motivations.

It is clear that discrimination, whether in relation to age and/or disability, is manifested in convoluted ways. Even within the respective groups of 'disabled' and 'old', some sub-groups are perceived and portrayed as being more 'other'. It is therefore imperative for these myriad similarities and differences, between and within groups, to be examined. This is especially pertinent in the run up to the launch of the CEHR in 2007 that takes a pan-equality approach by combining the different equality strands. The Commission must tread the careful balance of maintaining a cross-strand perspective while not losing sight of particular strand-specific issues. Hence the complex and often overlapping forms of discrimination must be mapped out and studied so that strategies can (hopefully) be formulated to tackle them in a consistent manner cognizant of similarities and differences in which such forces operate and are manifested within and across groups.

REFERENCES

d'Abbs, P. (1982) Social support networks: a critical review of models and findings, *Institute of Family Studies Monograph* No. 1, Melbourne, Australia: Institute of Family Studies.

Alibhai-Brown, Y. (1998) Age of respect, *Community Care*, 10–16 December, 24–5.

Arber, S. and Ginn, J. (1991) *Gender and Later Life: A Sociological Analysis of Resources and Constraints*, London: Sage.

Bardasi, E., Jenkins, S. and Rigg, J. (2000) *Disability, Work and Income: A British Perspective*, Institute for Social and Economic Research, Colchester: University of Essex.

BBC (2004) Call for right to independent living, 4 March, British Broadcasting Corporation (available at: http://news.bbc.co.uk/ 1/hi/uk/3529473.stm).

Campbell, J. (2004) A speech given at the DRC independent living public debate, 2 March, London.

Cooper, H., Arber, S., Fee, L. and Ginn, J. (1999) *The Influence of Social Support and Social Capital on Health: A Review and Analysis of British Data,* London: Health Education Authority.

DWP (2005) *Opportunity Age*, London: Department for Work and Pensions.

DoH (2004) *People Registered as Deaf or Hard of Hearing: Year Ending 31 March 2004, England*, London: Department of Health.

DRC (2001) *The DRC 2001: Attitudes and Awareness Survey*, London: Disability Rights Commission.

DRC (2002) *The DRC 2002: Attitudes and Awareness Survey*, London: Disability Rights Commission.

DRC (2003a) *The DRC 2003: Attitudes and Awareness Survey*, London: Disability Rights Commission.

DRC (2003b) The experiences of disabled people: the nature and extent of discrimination, *DRC Strategic Review*, London: Disability Rights Commission.

DRC (2003c) *Coming Together: Mental Health Service Users and Disability*, London: Disability Rights Commission.

DRC (2004) *Small Employers' Attitudes to Disability*, London: Disability Rights Commission.

DRC (2005a) *The 2011 Census: Initial View on Content for England and Wales. Response to Consultation on Possible Content of 2011 Census*, London: Disability Rights Commission.

DRC (2005b) *Disability Briefing, June 2005*, London: Disability Rights Commission.

DRC (2005c) *Shaping the Future of Equality*, London: Disability Rights Commission.

DRC (2006) *Are We Taking the Dis?* Campaign launch 30 January, London: Disability Rights Commission.

Disabled Persons' Transport Advisory Committee (2002) *Attitudes of Disabled People to Public Transport*, London: DPTAC.

Dowd, J. and Bengston, V. (1978) Aging in minority populations – an examination of the double jeopardy thesis, *Journal of Gerontology*, 33, 427–36.

Driver, S. and Martell, L. (1997) New Labour's communitarianisms, *Critical Social Policy,* 17(3), 27–44.

Easterbrook, L. (2003) *Moving on from Community Care. The Treatment, Care and Support of Older People in England*, London: Age Concern England.

Fennell, G., Phillipson, C. and Evers, H. (1988) *The Sociology of Old Age*, Buckingham: Open University Press.

Foong, A., Walsh, B., Goh, D. and Mann, S. (2000) Meeting the primary mental health care needs of elderly Chinese people in the UK: a case for specialist provision? *Mental Health Care*, 4(4), 130–33.

Gabriel, Z. and Bowling, A. (2004) Quality of life from the perspectives of older people, *Ageing and Society,* 24(5), 675–91.

Godfrey, M., Townsend, J. and Denby, T. (2004) *Building a Good Life for Older People in Local Communities*, York: Joseph Rowntree Foundation.

Goldberg, D.T. (1993) *Racist Culture: Philosophy and the Politics of Meaning*, Oxford: Blackwell.

Grewal, I., Joy, S., Lewis, J., Swales, K. and Woodfield, K. (2002) Disabled for life? Attitudes towards, and experiences of, disability in Britain, *Research Report 173,* Department for Work and Pensions.

Griffiths, R. (1988) *Community Care: Agenda for Action*, London: HMSO.

Harper, S. and Thane, P. (1989) The consolidation of 'old age' as a phase of life, 1945–1965, in Jefferys, M. (ed.) *Growing Old in the Twentieth Century*, London: Routledge, 43–61.

Johnson, N. (1999) The personal social services and community care, in Powell, M. (ed.) *New Labour, New Welfare State?* Bristol: The Policy Press, 77–100.

Laing and Buisson (2001) *Care of the Elderly Market Survey*, 14th edition, London: Laing and Buisson.

Modood, T., Berthoud, R., Lakey, J., Nazroo, J., Smith, P., Virdee, S. and Beishon, S. (1997) *Ethnic Minorities in Britain: Diversity and Disadvantage*. The fourth national survey of ethnic minorities, London: Policy Studies Institute.

ONS (2004) *Living in Britain 2002: General Household Survey*, London: Office for National Statistics.

Phillipson, C. (1982) *Capitalism and the Construction of Old Age*, London: Macmillan.

Priestley, M. (2000) Adults only: disability, social policy and the life course, *Journal of Social Policy*, 29(3), 421–39.

Priestley, M. (2002) *From Womb to Tomb*, Leeds: Centre for Disability Studies, University of Leeds.

Raj, D. (2003) *Where Are You From? Middle Class Migrants in the Modern World,* Berkeley: University of California Press.

Robinson, J. and Banks, P. (2005) *The Business of Caring: Kings Fund Inquiry into Care Services for Older People*, London: Kings Fund.

RNID (2005) *Deaf and Hard of Hearing People*, London: Royal National Institute for the Deaf.

Sin, C.H. (2004a) Communicating interviews: the experience of research with minority ethnic older people in Britain, *Quality in Ageing,* 5(2), 21–9.

Sin, C.H. (2004b) Sampling minority ethnic groups in Britain, *Ageing and Society,* 24(2), 257–77.

Sin, C.H. (2006) Expectations of support among white-British and Asian-Indian older people in Britain: the interdependence of formal and informal spheres, *Health and Social Care in the Community,* 14(3), 215–24.

Social Exclusion Unit (2004) *Mental Health and Social Exclusion,* London: Social Exclusion Unit.

Tester, S., Hubbard, G., Downs, M., MacDonald, C. and Murphy, J. (2004) Frailty and institutional life, in Walker, A. and Hennessy, C.H. (eds), *Growing Older. Quality of Life in Old Age,* Maidenhead: Open University Press, 209–24.

The Strategy Unit (2005) *Improving the Life Chances of Disabled People,* London: HMSO.

Tinker, A. (1997) *Older People in Modern Society,* 4th edition, London: Longman.

Townsend, P. (1981) The structural dependency of the elderly: the creation of social policy in the twentieth century, *Ageing and Society,* 1(1), 5–28.

Traynor, A. and Walker, A. (2003) People aged 65 and over. Results of a study carried out on behalf of the Department of Health as part of the 2001 General Household Survey, London: ONS.

Twomey, B., Nocon, A., Clark, J., Sin, C.H. and Sayce, L. (2005) Disability definitions and estimates, *Disability Rights Commission Internal Briefing Paper,* London: Disability Rights Commission.

Walker, A. (1980) The social creation of poverty and dependency in old age, *Journal of Social Policy,* 9(1), 49–75.

Ward, G. (1997) *Making Headlines: Mental Health and the National Press,* London: Health Education Authority.

Zarb, G. and Oliver, M. (1993) *Ageing With a Disability: What Do They Expect After All These Years,* London: University of Greenwich.

6

CONCLUSION

RICHARD WARD AND BILL BYTHEWAY

The Equality Act 2006 has led to the establishment in the UK of a Commission for Equality and Human Rights that will 'work towards the elimination of prejudice against, hatred of and hostility towards members of groups, and work towards enabling members of groups to participate in society'. It explains that the word 'group' here refers to a group or class of persons who share a common attribute in respect of any of the following: age, disability, gender, reassignment of gender, race, religion or belief, or sexual orientation. Thus the Act establishes an aim that relates a group and 'society'. There is however no acknowledgement that groups of people may share several of these attributes, and that this may generate prejudice, hatred and hostility within such groups. Thus the matter of multiple discrimination is overlooked.

To support the implementation of the Act, Tony Blair (as prime minister) commissioned a review and, in February 2007, 'Fairness and Freedom: The Final Report of the Equalities Review' was published. Regarding multiple discrimination, it includes the following sceptical comments:

The phrase 'multiple disadvantage' has drifted into popular use in recent years. It is taken to mean that having more than one characteristic typically associated with a disadvantage increases an individual's likelihood of experiencing that disadvantage. The idea has even been lampooned with some media competing to find the most 'oppressed' person – the fabled Black disabled lesbian, for example. But research shows that the concept does have some validity when considering employment.

Multiple markers of disadvantages can drastically reduce the probability of being employed. For instance, disabled people have very low rates of employment when their disability is accompanied by other factors, such as lone parenthood, belonging to an ethnic minority group or a lack of educational qualifications. Pakistani and Bangladeshi women are more likely to have three additional disadvantaging characteristics other than ethnicity: having young children, lower educational qualifications and living in an area with relatively high unemployment rates.

However, evidence suggests that this is not a simple phenomenon and is only true in a few special cases. (pp 72–3)

The evidence cited by the Review refers exclusively to employment and is based on an analysis of statistical comparisons and trends over time rather than how people experience multiple discrimination. There is no serious attention given for example to how black disabled lesbians might react to being lampooned in the media. There is an implicit assumption that the distinctive experiences of such people need not concern the Commission. This is evidence of a reluctance in policy development to acknowledge, and respond to, complexity in discrimination.

The newly established Commission for Equality and Human Rights however now claims on its website (September 2007), that a single commission will have many benefits including 'giving older people a powerful national body to tackle age discrimination' and 'tackling discrimination on multiple levels – some people may face more than one type of discrimination' (CEHR 2007). Thus it would appear that policy is beginning to 'tackle' the kinds of discrimination that people over retirement age might experience.

INTERSECTIONALITY

The Equality Act is referenced specifically to: age, disability, gender, race, religion or belief, and sexual orientation (and reassignment of gender). These are sometimes referred to as the six 'strands' to the new anti-discrimination legislation being developed on the basis of Article 13 of the 1997 Amsterdam Treaty of the European Union. It has been claimed that this Article reflects a shared desire to make the most of joint efforts to combat discrimination, to benefit from transfers of experience and good practice across the various strands, and to provide a more effective basis for addressing situations of multiple discrimination (European Commission 2004).

The overall aim is that under certain prescribed conditions, discrimination should be legally actionable, thereby protecting older people among others against unfair discrimination. The goal of 'fairness for all' however raises many questions. Already there is concern that debates are being shaped by a legislative focus, and that too much hangs upon legal interpretation and the setting of precedents. For example, McCrudden (2005: 18) argues that an individual justice model concentrates on the intention of the perpetrator of discrimination and on the victim's possible sense of grievance. Furthermore, defining discrimination in relation to wider principles of equality encourages assumptions of equivalence between the six strands, potentially creating competition between their respective advocates and, arguably, failing to address the need for a more structural approach to tackling inequality (McCrudden 2003; Verloo 2006). There is every prospect that coverage of the various strands will differ under the law and that the significance of intersecting forms of discrimination will continue to be neglected (Fredman 2005). In other words, the worrying prospect is that, following the Equalities Act, further anti-discrimination legislation will separate out different types of prejudice in an attempt to tackle each in isolation.

In order to draw attention to multiple discrimination and evade political conflict between competing groups, Crenshaw introduced the notion of intersectionality (1994). She defines this as 'intersecting patterns of racism and sexism' in order to explain the ways in which sex discrimination law has focused upon white women and race discrimination law on black men. This generated much interest in studies of racism and sexism, and in the development of anti-discrimination policies (see Yuval-Davis 2006), but little in relation to examples of other kinds of intersection. For example Essed (2001), in discussing intersectionality, focuses primarily upon race and gender. Age figures but only in consolidating accounts of discrimination. For example she discusses two cases of race-related sexual harassment where age is seen as oppressing youth. In the first, a 'white male in his 50s' harasses 'an African-American student, aged 19'. In the second, concerning a white male professor and a black woman student, age difference is only made explicit in the student's response:

> Angry that he abuses the situation, is 'older' and 'not at all attractive', she pushes him away with a decisive 'NO'.

Arguably, the middle clause of this key sentence is evidence of younger people expressing prejudicial 'hostility' towards people who are 'older'.

More recently however, there has been a growing recognition that intersectionality is relevant to understanding how *all* forms of discrimination are amplified as they interact and coalesce. Phoenix and Pattynama (2006: 187), for example, argue that intersectionality is fast becoming 'useful as a handy catchall phrase that aims to make visible the multiple positioning that constitutes everyday life and the power relations that are central to it'.

With age discrimination currently still a contested and problematic term, there is good reason to consider ways of understanding ageism and ageist discrimination beyond the courtroom and its focus upon overt, extreme, and thereby actionable, practices. Attention to the experience of discrimination in later life offers alternative but no less powerful insights and bears comparison with explorations of the experience of prejudice from other standpoints.

This collection of papers has addressed issues hanging over those who face multiple and interlocking discriminations. In their different ways, each of the papers locates discrimination in a context that is all too easily overlooked by definitions and concerns derived from policy and legislation. They draw upon experiences reported by older people, revealing how these are a rich source of insights into the complex nature of multiple discrimination.

DISCRIMINATION AND EVERYDAY EXPERIENCES

Essed has led the way in developing a theoretical account of everyday discrimination (1991). In developing her theory of everyday racism, she draws upon black and migrant women's firsthand knowledge of discrimination, and sets out what is for us a compelling argument for the scrutiny of familiar and mundane encounters, rather than exceptional experiences where evidence of discrimination appears indisputable. She concludes that systemic racism is reproduced largely through routine and taken-for-granted practices and procedures in everyday life; that it is often hard to pinpoint and therefore to challenge; and that every new experience resonates and reconfigures the accumulation of earlier events. This last feature of everyday discrimination is particularly relevant in understanding and interpreting later life experiences.

A focus on the everyday however has led to criticisms that different types of social process and phenomena are conflated and addressed on only one level of analysis: the experiential. Essed (2001) has felt obliged to defend her approach:

> As a concept everyday racism has been useful in showing that systemic racism is reproduced largely through routine and taken-for-granted practices and procedures in everyday life. This does not make everyday racism a problem of a more humane kind. Although everyday racism has such an informal ring that it may sound as it if concerns relatively harmless and unproblematic events, the psychological distress due to racism on a day-to-day basis can have chronic adverse effects on mental and physical health.

It is interesting that she claims here that the threat of everyday racism is the emergence of chronic ill-health as a consequence of the slow accumulation of racist experiences rather than an impoverished and demoralised old age. In this respect she reflects how much of the debate over intersectionality has overlooked the long-term significance of the continuing and accumulating experience of discrimination.

EVERYDAY AGEISM AND AGE DISCRIMINATION

Nevertheless, drawing heavily upon her approach in analysing our own research evidence, we have developed the following definition of everyday ageism:

> Everyday ageism does not exist as single event but as a complex of cumulative practices. Specific instances acquire meaning only in relation to the accumulating total of other experiences of everyday ageism. It involves ageist practices that infiltrate everyday life and are part of what is popularly seen as 'normal'. Analogous to everyday life, everyday ageism is heterogeneous in its manifestations but, at the same time, unified by the constant repetition of particular practices.
>
> (Bytheway *et al.* 2007: 94)

This leads us to define age discrimination in the following way:

> Everyday age discrimination is a consequence of ageist practices. Because it is part of everyday experience, reinforced by mundane and commonplace practices, everyday age discrimination is rarely noticed. Discrimination is only noticed when it is experienced as something that is 'out of the ordinary'.

It is not difficult to see in the papers in this collection evidence of everyday age discrimination. In particular, the slow accumulation of many, seemingly minor, humiliations explains the long process of exclusion and withdrawal from public places and intergenerational social relations. A focus on 'everyday' experience encompasses a broad spectrum of forms and expressions of prejudice and discriminatory action. Everything and anything that might be encountered on a day to day basis can be examined as evidence of discrimination.

All four papers draw attention to the fluid and contingent nature of discrimination and the identities or positionings associated with it. In contrast to the great act of disentanglement currently underway in formulating anti-discrimination policy, these papers underline how age connects with the other structural dimensions to which the legislation refers. Age is culturally produced and reiterated in ways that are shaped by time and place. In this way identities are 'en-aged' and the experience of growing older is made complex and diverse.

RESEARCHING AGEING AND MULTIPLE DISCRIMINATION

We began this report with the suggestion that discrimination in later life warrants greater critical attention than it is currently afforded. Each chapter lends fuel to the argument that discrimination is a daily fact of life for older people and inhabits even the most fleeting social encounter. The routine and repeated quality of discrimination is underlined; a process that naturalises dominant messages about old age. The cultural processes that uphold inequality have been explored, foregrounding the patterns of daily living: a visit to the hairdressers; a trip to the swimming pool; a drink in a bar; or a GP consultation. Embedded within such ordinary events are the politics of ageing and intersections with varied social divisions.

∴ need AMA to look @ the
"something new" in employment
discrim

Our concern with multiple discrimination signals a critique of rights-based legislation that upholds divisions such as 'race', gender, sexual orientation and age. The papers presented here underline the permeability of these 'strands' and generate questions regarding what might be involved in challenging multiple discrimination. Importantly, the evidence on offer highlights the reductionism behind additive notions of discrimination, where the perceived effect of one brand of prejudice is layered upon the next. Where different forms of discrimination intersect, something new emerges that is yet to be well understood. At present, we have the 'catch-all phrase' intersectionality, but the debate surrounding it is guilty of neglecting age. One aim of this volume is to consider how attention to ageing and the involvement of older people might generate insights and shed light on previously overlooked aspects of inequality. Consequently, it is made clear that older people must take centre stage in the effort to define and understand discrimination in later life.

The chapters in this report serve to challenge assumptions that discrimination happens only in particular settings; is attributable to certain people; confined to certain types of relationship or can be pinned down to particular practices. In short, discrimination is not predictable: we cannot always tell easily when it has occurred, or how to remedy it. Much of the experience described in this report concerns what is ordinary and thereby unlikely to warrant judicial scrutiny. The chapters combine to reveal that discrimination is heterogeneous in its forms and effects, cumulative in the context of people's lives, pervasive and contingent. The gathered evidence suggests much discrimination is experienced as subtle and even ambiguous. As we have seen, there can be uncertainty surrounding how to make sense of a particular encounter, or in being sure what motives lay behind the conduct of others. As Sin highlights in Chapter 5, the fixed and robust categories on which policy, planning and research rely are lived very differently, they are often thought about and negotiated in far less definite or deliberate ways. Life rarely separates out into neat categories that remain fixed and unchanging.

Despite this diffuse quality to multiple identities, the points where they intersect and overlap remain largely unexplored. As Sin (Chapter 5) goes on to remind us, divisions govern research and policy in ways that seem artificial and even irrelevant to how we define ourselves or are labelled by others. And, when research intervenes in older people's lives it creates intersections of ageing with these other divisions, even as it sets out to question them. Research into ageing is productive, how else would focus groups on racism and age discrimination in neighbouring cities lead to contrasting emphases, or interviews concerning sexuality and ageing elicit markedly different discussions on discrimination? The generative and constructive role played by research is therefore itself a consideration in understanding discrimination.

In Chapter 4 the relationship of the research process to its outcomes is usefully highlighted. The authors consider the way methods of recruitment can dictate the sort of people who participate. At present, it is rarely acknowledged that many individuals most readily identified as 'older', 'gay/lesbian', 'disabled' are often activists, and populate research in numbers not fully recognised. How well they represent a wider population is difficult to estimate. The older person is someone we assume to know. But as the evidence gathered here illustrates, many people reject the label of 'old', it is an unwanted subject position from which to speak, a point often ignored by policy makers, service providers and researchers alike. As Sin predicts, it is a condition that holds implications for the success of a rights-based agenda: if people are reluctant to subscribe to the category of 'old' on what basis will oppression be challenged or opposition mobilised. Of course, a major reason for this is discrimination. Those who embrace old age might be considered activists on this basis.

The standpoint of the activist is therefore well represented in the research detailed here and it behoves us to end this report with a consideration of what this might mean. Having heard from people with a capacity to recognise, interpret and articulate discriminatory encounters, perhaps this indicates that activism helps people learn how to make sense of their experiences. If this is so, and activism provides a language and framework both for understanding discrimination, and a repertoire of strategies for challenging it then we might usefully make their presence in research better known. As this report confirms, while some people accept the dominant and largely negative messages related to old age others question and challenge that message. In this challenge lies the road to a more age inclusive society.

REFERENCES

Bytheway, B., Ward, R., Holland, C. and Peace, S. (2007) *Too Old: Older People's Accounts of Discrimination, Exclusion and Rejection*, London: Help the Aged.

CEHR (2007) http://www.cehr.org.uk/content/purpose.rhtm

Crenshaw, K.W. (1994) Mapping the margins: intersectionality, identity politics and violence against women of color, in Fineman, M.A. and Mykitiuk, R. (eds) *The Public Nature of Private Violence*, New York: Routledge, pp. 93–118.

Essed, P. (1991) *Understanding Everyday Racism: an Interdisciplinary Theory*, Newbury Park, CA: Sage.

Essed, P. (2001) Towards a methodology to identify converging forms of everyday discrimination, at www.un.org/womenwatch/daw/csw/essed45.htm

European Commission (2004) *Equality and Non-Discrimination in an Enlarged European Union*, Directorate-General for Employment and Social Affairs.

Fredman, S. (2005) Double trouble: multiple discrimination and EU law, *European Anti-Discrimination Law Review*, 2, 13–21.

McCrudden, C. (2003) 'The New Concept of Equality', *Fight Against Discrimination: The Race and Framework Employment Directive*, Academy of European Law, Trier, June 2003.

McCrudden, C. (2005) Thinking about the Discrimination Directives, *European Anti-Discrimination Law Review*, 1, 17–23.

Phoenix, A. and Pattynama, P. (2006) Intersectionality, *European Journal of Women's Studies*, 13, 187–92.

Verloo, M. (2006) Multiple inequalities, intersectionality and the European Union, *European Journal of Women's Studies*, 13, 211–28.

Yuval-Davis, N. (2006) Intersectionality and feminist politics, *European Journal of Women's Studies*, 13, 193–209.

ABOUT THE AUTHORS

Bill Bytheway is a Senior Research Fellow in the Faculty of Health and Social Care at the Open University.

Caroline Holland is a Research Associate in the Faculty of Health and Social Care at the Open University.

Chih Hoong Sin was Head of Information and Research for the Disability Rights Commission, London until September 2007 and is currently an independent consultant.

Jonathan Hughes is a Lecturer in the Centre for Widening Participation at the Open University.

Nicola Humberstone works to 'Improve the Patient Experience' for Services for Older People in Tower Hamlets PCT, is the development worker with older lesbians for the Association of Greater London Older Women, and is doing research on LGBTs in soap operas.

Rebecca Jones is a Lecturer (Health and Social Care) in the Faculty of Health and Social Care at the Open University.

Rosalind Pearson has worked and campaigned with the National Pensioners Convention, devised the *Exploring Living Memory* media event and exhibition, and produced several television documentaries about older women.

Anthea Symonds is an independent consultant researcher, an Associate Lecturer for the Open University and an Adult Education Lecturer at Swansea University.

Richard Ward is a Research Fellow in the Centre for the Older Person's Agenda (COPA) at Queen Margaret University, Edinburgh.